BFI Modern Classics

Rob White
Series Editor

Advancing into its second century, the cinema is now a mature art form with an established list of classics. But contemporary cinema is so subject to every shift in fashion regarding aesthetics, morals and ideas that judgments on the true worth of recent films are liable to be risky and controversial; yet they are essential if we want to know where the cinema is going and what it can achieve.

As part of the British Film Institute's commitment to the promotion and evaluation of contemporary cinema, and in conjunction with the influential BFI Film Classics series, BFI Modern Classics is a series of books devoted to individual films of recent years. Distinguished film critics, scholars and novelists explore the production and reception of their chosen films in the context of an argument about the film's importance. Insightful, considered, often impassioned, these elegant, beautifully illustrated books will set the agenda for debates about what matters in modern cinema.

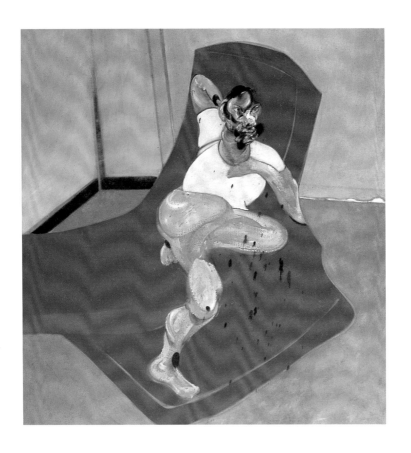

Left panel of Double Portrait of Lucien Freud and Frank Auerbach, 1964
(Moderna Museet, Stockholm)

BFI MODERN CLASSICS

Last Tango in Paris

**David
Thompson**

 Publishing

First published in 1998 by the
British Film Institute
21 Stephen Street, London W1P 2LN

The British Film Institute exists to promote
appreciation, enjoyment, protection and
development of moving image culture in and
throughout the whole of the United Kingdom.
Its activities include the National Film and
Television Archive; the National Film Theatre;
the Museum of the Moving Image;
the London Film Fesival; the production and
distribution of film and video; funding and
support for regional activities; Library and
Information Services; Stills, Posters and
Designs; Research; Publishing and Education;
and the monthly *Sight and Sound* magazine.

Series design by Andrew Barron &
Collis Clements Associates

Typeset in Italian Garamond
by D R Bungay Associates, Burghfield, Berks

Picture editing by Liz Heasman

Designed by Tom Cabot and Rob White

Printed in Great Britain by
Norwich Colour Print, Drayton, Norfolk

British Library Cataloguing-in-Publication Data
A catalogue record for this book is available
from the British Library
ISBN 0-85170-545-6

Contents

This must be the most powerfully erotic movie ever made.

Pauline Kael

The bourgeois West knows no other vital truth save that of sex. All the rest is macabre parody.

Alberto Moravia

I don't think Bertolucci knew what the film was about. And I didn't know what it was about. ... He looks at me one day and he says, you know ... something like, 'You are the embodiment, or reincarnation ... you are the ... symbol of my prick'. I mean, what the fuck does that mean?

Marlon Brando

Why does Marlon Brando use butter for his sexual feat? It's so expensive.

Woman interviewed outside a Paris cinema after seeing *Last Tango in Paris*

Acknowledgments

Francis Bacon's 'Double Portrait of Lucien Freud and Frank Auerbach, 1964' (Freud panel only), in the Moderna Museet, Stockholm, and 'Study for Portrait (Isabel Rawsthorne), 1964', in private collection; both copyright Francis Bacon Estate.

For their support and assistance, thanks are due to Geoff Andrew, Kate Austin (Marlborough Fine Art), John Baxter, Hercules Belville, Paul Kerr, David Meeker, Chris Rodley, Paul Ryan, Markku Salmi, Marina Warner, the staff of the British Film Institute Library and of course Ed Buscombe and Rob White of BFI Publishing. A special 'thank you' also to Bernardo Bertolucci for his generosity and patience.

1 The Production

In my lifetime, few films have created such an intense climate of
expectation as did *Last Tango in Paris* on its release in Britain in March
1973. It was the work of a thirty-one-year-old Italian director, made in
French and English, starred one of the great icons of American cinema
and – the decisive factor – contained (reportedly) outrageous sex scenes.
Over the years, the furore has died away, but the film itself, in its
complexities, its contradictions and its excesses, still has the power to
provoke and reward the spectator.

The basic story of *Last Tango* is simple to recount. A forty-five-year-
old ex-patriate American named Paul (Marlon Brando) and a twenty-
year-old French bourgeoise named Jeanne (Maria Schneider) meet in an
empty apartment in Paris, and almost instantaneously have sex. They
part, but are drawn together for further encounters, isolated in a private
world in which they neither seek to know the other's name nor their
past, and in which they break society's taboos. Most notably these
include sodomy with the use of butter as a lubricant. But Paul, we learn
outside of the apartment, is in despair over the mysterious suicide of his
wife Rosa, the owner of a seedy hotel he continues to run. Jeanne is
engaged to a young film-maker named Tom (Jean-Pierre Léaud), who
turns his camera on her to portray her life and their love. Eventually the
'real' lives of Paul and Jeanne disrupt their secret mutual obsession.
Though she declares that she loves Paul, Jeanne agrees to marry Tom.
When finally Paul feels liberated from his miserable past, he pursues
Jeanne outside the apartment, declaring his love for her and asking her
to live with him. But she is no longer interested in him, and just as she
finally tells him her name, she shoots him dead.

Last Tango was the first of Bernardo Bertolucci's films not to be a
literary adaptation. Like many of his generation, Bertolucci did not arrive
at film-making by serving his time in the industry. He was born 16 March
1941 in Baccanelli, near Parma in Northern Italy. His father, Attilio
Bertolucci, was an established poet as well as an art and film critic, and
the young Bernardo soaked up his love of literature and cinema. As a

teenager in Rome he was making modest 16mm shorts, and by the age of twenty had published a prize-winning collection of poems, *In ricerca del mistero* (*In Search of Mystery*). Through his father, he met Pier Paolo Pasolini, and joined the poet-turned-director as assistant on his first film, *Accattone* (1961), an intensely formative experience.

Bertolucci's first solo film, *La commare secca* (*The Grim Reaper,* 1962), was based on a story by Pasolini, and attracted good notices. But it was with his second film that Bertolucci emerged as a front runner in the rejuvenated European cinema of the early 60s. *Before the Revolution* (*Prima della rivoluzione*, 1964), loosely based on Stendahl's *The Charterhouse of Parma*, was an expression of Bertolucci's own inner contradictions, both in its focus on a young man torn between revolutionary ideals (the director himself joined the Italian Communist Party) and the pursuit of romantic love, and in its stylistic waverings between the swooning camera of Max Ophuls and the jagged editing of Jean-Luc Godard. It also spoke of love of cinema for itself – or to use that tainted word, cinephilia – and featured an extended dance sequence, two elements which would recur in *Last Tango*.

Despite great critical acclaim – particularly in the USA – *Before the Revolution* was a commercial flop. Bertolucci's subsequent film, *Partner* (1968), was more experimental, and in its fractured visuals and soundtrack delivered a challenge to the audience which they received with indifference. But it did feature Bertolucci's first tango, when Pierre Clementi crashes a society party and parodies the guests by performing a solo dance. The international acclaim of five years earlier returned with two festival hits: *The Spider's Stratagem* (*Strategia del ragno*, 1970), a visually elaborate (despite its TV origins) Oedipal tale based on a Jorge Luis Borges story of a son discovering the complex truth about his 'heroic' father; and *The Conformist* (*Il conformista*, 1970), based on an Alberto Moravia novel.

The Conformist begins in 30s Fascist Italy and moves to Paris by following Marcello Clerici (Jean-Louis Trintignant) on a mission to assassinate his former professor, who is regarded as a subversive by the right-wing friends Clerici wishes to impress. Bertolucci uses this framework to explore the psycho-sexual problems of the main character; by now the director was seeing a psychoanalyst regularly and was totally absorbed by the discoveries he was making. Clerici is troubled both by a homosexual encounter in his youth, as well as his obsession with the professor's young wife Anna (Dominique Sanda). In an exhilaratingly choreographed sequence in a dance hall, Anna performs a provocative tango with Clerici's daffy new bride (Stefania Sandrelli). If anyone had doubts about Bertolucci's ripe talent, they were now cast aside. In its bold stylistic surface – extreme colour schemes, tilted angles, swooning camera movements, dynamic cutting – the film announced the arrival of the Italian 'dream team' of cinematographer Vittorio Storaro, production designer Ferdinando Scarfiotti, editor and co-writer Franco 'Kim' Arcalli and their youthful director.

Given his fascination with American cinema, it was inevitable that the ambitious young director would seek to make a film in the USA. His

The Conformist – another tango in Paris

chosen subject was Dashiell Hammett's novel *Red Harvest*. But for his next Italian project, he planned to make a political epic, *Novecento* (*1900*). These were both works in progress when a further idea began to preoccupy him. As Bertolucci later described it, the genesis of *Last Tango* lay in his desire 'to meet a woman in an empty apartment without knowing who that territory belonged to and to make love with her without knowing who she was. I'd like to meet again and again without asking or being asked any questions. *Last Tango* is the development of this very personal and perhaps banal obsession.'[1]

During the last part of the shooting of *The Conformist*, I had an encounter with a woman. It was not at all like the one between Marlon and Maria, but because I felt a bit guilty about it at the time, in my fantasy I made it an encounter with an unknown woman. As I was feeling I would like to have a change in my life – I had been living with a woman [Maria Paola Maino, an antiques dealer who was also his set designer] for a long time, perhaps six years – a way of making this switch happen in my life was to represent it first in a movie.

I started to think about a movie called *Un giorno, una notte, un giorno, una notte – A Day and a Night, A Day and a Night* – and this was the first version of *Last Tango in Paris*. I wrote a page or a page and a half. Actually, the first draft was set in Milan, so it could have been *Last Tango in Milan*! In the second draft, I moved the story to Paris, and gave it the title *La Petite morte*, which is the eighteenth-century Libertine expression for orgasm. I was reading a lot of Georges Bataille, including *Le Bleu du ciel*, which really impressed me. When later on, in 1976, in Cannes I saw Nagisa Oshima's *L'Empire des sens*, I found it very close to *Last Tango* in some ways, and not because *Last Tango* had influenced Nagisa, but because we were both influenced by Bataille. I remember a scene in the script, which I didn't shoot, which came directly from *Le Bleu du ciel*; it is a moment when the lovers are so obsessed with the shell of their love, she says she would like to open a window and he says, 'No, no, no, I want to breathe the air on our breath, when we fart or when we come' – it was the idea of keeping something to themselves. So even if I say that *Last Tango* was the first of my films not taken from a novel or a short story, nevertheless I think there was the benevolent shadow of a book protecting me.

Georges Bataille's *Le Bleu du ciel*, translated as *Blue of Noon*, was written in 1935 but not published until 1957 because, the author felt, the events of the early 30s against which the story unfolds – revolution among the working classes, the rise of Fascism – had been rendered insignificant by the Spanish Civil War and the Second World War. Told in the first person, the central character is a disenchanted, wealthy European man who travels from one hotel room to another (including the Savoy!), and from one lover to another. Although there are no obvious plot similarities to *Last Tango*, the encounters in enclosed spaces have a comparable erotic charge, a circumscribed environment in which the orgasmic urge is inextricable from the harshly physical and the sordid.

In his essay 'A Transit to Narcissus', published as an afterword to the screenplay of *Last Tango*, Norman Mailer offered an example of dialogue from an early version of the script, in which the Paul character is named Leon.

LEON: I make you die, you make me die, we're two murderers, each other's. But who succeeds in this is twice the murderer. And that's the biggest pleasure: watching you die, watching you come out of yourself, white-eyed, writhing, gasping, screaming so loud that it seems like the last time.

While it arguably loses in translation, the ghost of Bataille hovers over these lines, and there is (blissfully) a huge leap from this style of language to that of the finished film, much of it down to the casting. As is well known, Bertolucci's original idea was to reunite the two lead actors from *The Conformist*, Jean-Louis Trintignant and Dominique Sanda, as the anonymous lovers, but there were problems ahead.

Trintignant is beyond shyness, and he couldn't be *à poil*, meaning naked, in front of the camera – he was almost crying when he told me that. Dominique was pregnant by Christian Marquand, so she was not available either. For the man, I then went to see both Jean-Paul Belmondo and Alain Delon, who were the two French actors of the moment. Belmondo really didn't care for it, he thought it was a piece of obscenity. Delon liked it very much, and said, 'I am ready to do it tomorrow, but I want to be the producer of the film'. But I thought it was impossible to accept the power a producer has over a film coinciding with him playing the protagonist.

I was in Rome having dinner, and among the guests was Luigi Luraschi from the Italian office of Paramount. Marlon Brando's name came up, and I said, 'yeah, that's the one'. Because I could see a way of going away from a love story between two young people, which I didn't think was right. The script was still very much a work in progress then. And Luigi Luraschi knew Marlon quite well, so he called him, and a week later Marlon flew to Paris, where I met him. He wanted to see *The Conformist*. I asked him why, and he said a friend of his had told him it was a fantastic film, and he trusted their judgment. I found out some months later that Marlon's friend was a Chinese lady called Anita [Anita Kong, a long-time lover of Brando].

I remember taking Marlon to lunch at the Hotel Raphael, where Rossellini used to stay, and then going to see *The Conformist*. At the end he said, 'OK, what's the movie you want to do about?' I told him, and we met the day after. My English was bad, but I discovered that Marlon could speak French, a very naïve, sweet Tahitian French. If I'm not understandable in English today, I always say it's thanks to my first teacher, Marlon Brando, who no-one could understand because of his mumbling!

In the summer of 1971 I worked with Kim Arcalli, and then my brother Guiseppe, and in a month or so we wrote the script. Kim was older than me, so he was closer to Marlon's character. Kim was also a very wild character, extremely fascinating, self-taught – his university was the partisan war, and at fifteen he was pretending to be twenty. But having cast Marlon, it helped us a great deal to focus the story. I was supposed to shoot at the beginning of the fall, but Marlon summoned me to go to Los Angeles to talk about the film. It was my first trip there; I stayed at the Beverly Hills Hotel, and he was where he still lives in Mulholland Drive. I spent about three weeks with him, but we never talked about the film, instead we talked about everything else – life and death, girls, the usual.

At this stage Paramount, the studio who were financing the development of the project, dropped out; ironically enough, they had no confidence in Brando's box-office appeal, as *The Godfather* was still in the cutting

(Overleaf) Brando and Bertolucci on set

room. But Bertolucci met the President of United Artists in New York, David Picker, who after listening to the proposed story in a matter of minutes agreed to a budget of a million dollars. As a completion bond guarantee was needed, which Bertolucci's producer cousin Giovanni could not raise, the director approached Alberto Grimaldi, who had already secured the rights for *Red Harvest* for him. Grimaldi's credits as a producer already included Sergio Leone's *The Good, the Bad, and the Ugly* (1966), Gillo Pontecorvo's *Queimada!* (*Burn!*, 1968), and Federico Fellini's *Satyricon* (1969) and *Roma* (1972). Grimaldi had recently sued Brando for $700,000 for his 'incomprehensible attitude' and 'open hostility' towards Pontecorvo on *Queimada!*, in which the actor had played the lead role. But for his participation in *Last Tango*, Grimaldi told Brando's agent he would settle the case and pay the actor $250,000 plus 10 per cent of the gross above a take of $3 million. Brando accepted the terms.

The casting for the role of Jeanne was only resolved late in the day. It was constantly reported that a number of leading French actresses rejected the part because of the sexual explicitness of the script. Although one name often mentioned was Catherine Deneuve, like Sanda she was pregnant and therefore not available. Bertolucci later said, 'If Deneuve had played the part, I would have pushed Marlon to dirty the kind of bourgeois innocence that she always projects.'[2] In fact, Bertolucci was looking at many young actresses (some reports said 200, but it was nearer fifty). Finally he focused on two unknown women for the part, who he screen-tested. One was Aurore Clement, who in the director's words 'looked like an angel, with her curly hair' (she later appeared in Louis Malle's *Lacombe Lucien* (1973) and Chantal Akerman's *Les Rendezvous d'Anna* (1978)). The other was Maria Schneider. According to the director, he finally chose Schneider because he saw her working better with Brando.

At the beginning of 1972, a trade announcement revealed the final deal on the film, which by this stage was an Italian-French co-production, but financed through the USA. The budget was set at $1,200,000, with United Artists holding world rights. Filming commenced in Paris on 31

January, with Brando joining the unit a week later on 7 February. After ten weeks of filming, the production wrapped on 15 April, slightly over schedule.

2 The Reception

When I saw the first complete cut of *Last Tango*, my editor Kim Arcalli and myself thought,'Who will go to see such a tragic, desperate film?' We then looked to our producer, Alberto Grimaldi, thinking he would be sad and pessimistic, but he was dancing for joy. We asked him why, and he said, 'Because this film has an incredible impact.'

Whatever their differing personal feelings, Grimaldi and Bertolucci must have realised as the editing on *Last Tango* progressed through the summer of 1972 that their film was going to be exceptionally controversial. As he had always received strong support in New York, Bertolucci opted for a world premiere at the New York Film Festival, an annual event then held in October. The tenth Festival's line-up shows these were golden years for 'art' cinema, with new films by Eric Rohmer, François Truffaut, Bob Rafelson, Ken Loach, Rainer Werner Fassbinder and Luis Buñuel, whose *Le Charme discret de la bourgeoisie* (*The Discreet Charm of the Bourgeoisie*, 1972) would be one of the biggest foreign language hits of the time.

But the hottest ticket of all was the closing night attraction, *Last Tango in Paris*, to be screened once only. Unusually, no press show could be held; the reason given was that since the film was, in business terms, an Italian production, it had to be shown to the Italian censors prior to a world screening, or else forfeit its subsidy from the home box office. United Artists and Alberto Grimaldi obtained dispensation for a single screening under strict security, which literally meant the print was escorted by armed guards. This followed a precedent set that same year by the Berlin Film Festival's screening of Pasolini's *The Canterbury Tales* (1972), also a Grimaldi production. Like *Last Tango*, Pasolini's film tested the boundaries of sexual explicitness, and a good critical response (and in the case of the Pasolini film, a major prize to boot) would encourage a certain leniency on the censor's part. Not wanting to miss a trick, Grimaldi even flew in half a dozen selected Italian journalists for the New York screening.

On the night, the demand for tickets was unprecedentedly high. According to *Variety*, touts were asking anything up to $150 for a ticket, but few punters were willing to give up their place in history. Molly Haskel in *The Village Voice* noted the audience reaction as being highly divided: 'The gays, as a group, were the most negative; men of heterosexual persuasion either liked it with "strong reservations" or didn't like it at all. … Women were either negative, with an undertone of disapproval, or wildly partisan.' Haskell herself was definitely in the last group, acknowledging that

reactions by sex are probably justified because it is a film about sexual attraction, about an affair 'for sex only' (which ultimately disproves its very possibility), about de-repressing a woman, initiating her into all the low-down lusts and body needs in a relationship that, unlike those in [Henry] Miller and [D.H.] Lawrence and most eroticists, does as much – perhaps more – for the woman as for the man.[3]

Robert Altman, riding his own wave of fame following the success of *M*A*S*H* (1970), was bowled over by the film. 'I walked out of the screening and said to myself, "How dare I make another movie?" What it has done is give me a twenty year jump in my career. The level of honesty it achieved was fantastic – not the sexuality but the emotional honesty. My personal and artistic life will never be the same.'[4]

But unquestionably the highest – and loudest – praise for the film came from the diva of New York film critics, Pauline Kael. Her instant review in *The New Yorker* magazine was used as a major part of the film's publicity campaign – it subsequently filled two pages of the *Sunday New York Times*, paid for by United Artists. It was also the kind of rave which few films could hope to live up to.

Bernardo Bertolucci's *Last Tango in Paris* was presented for the first time on the closing night of the New York Film Festival, 14 October 1972; that date should become a landmark in movie history comparable to 29 May 1913 – the night 'Le Sacre du printemps' was first performed – in music history. There was no riot, and no-one threw anything at the screen, but I think it's fair to say that the audience was in a state of shock, because *Last Tango in Paris* has the same kind of hypnotic excitement as the 'Sacre', the same primitive force, the same thrusting jabbing eroticism.[5]

This sincere, if in retrospect misplaced analogy, was more than Norman Mailer could take. Six months later, he wrote of the opening sequence:

Abruptly Brando cashes the check Stanley Kowalski wrote for us twenty-five years ago – he fucks the heroine standing up. It solves the old snicker of how you do it in a telephone booth? – he rips her panties open. In our new line of *New Yorker*-approved superlatives, it can be said that the cry of the fabric is the most thrilling sound to be heard in world culture since the four opening notes of Beethoven's 'Fifth'.

Kael's bold stance, in combination with her being first in print, became a red rag to the bullish US critics. Reviewing the film now meant taking on Pauline at your peril. But *Last Tango* not only had every critic in the land scrambling to say something provocative, it also achieved a double whammy of cover stories in both *Newsweek* and *Time* magazines. You could even find stills of the nude scenes in the January issue of *Playboy*. Suddenly there wasn't a more fashionable movie for the critics either to laud to the skies or snidely put down. United Artists capitalised on all this heat by opening the film on 1 February 1973 at one screen on the East side of New York (the Trans Lux) and charging the higher than usual ticket price of $5, over which even the director expressed his misgivings (this figure carried particular connotations in New York, as the normal admission price to a movie theatre was then $3, and $5 was what one paid to see a 'top-class' pornographic film such as *Deep Throat*). The venue was sold out weeks in advance. But for all the showbiz bravado on display, corporate America was not so willing to be identified with such a dangerous film.

United Artists were actually shocked when they saw the film. At the time, the United Artists logo read 'United Artists – Entertainment from Transamerica

Corporation'. They removed the last part in the USA! It received an 'X' rating, as had *Midnight Cowboy* and *Carnal Knowledge*. And I believe it was after *Last Tango* that newspapers and magazines started objecting to advertising 'X' rated films.

Nevertheless, *Last Tango* went on to take $16 million at the US box office. The film opened in Italy in January 1973, and after running just one week, a private prosecution was brought by a citizen in Bologna, charging the film with (take a deep breath)

obscene content offensive to public decency, characterised by an extreme pansexualism for its own sake, presented with an obsessive self-indulgence catering to the lowest instincts of the libido, dominated by the idea of stirring unchecked appetites for sexual pleasure, permeated by scurrilous language, with crude repulsive, naturalistic and even unnatural representation of carnal union, with continued and complacent scenes, descriptions and exhibitions of masturbation, libidinous acts and lewd nudity, accompanied off-screen by sounds, sighs, and shrieks of climactic pleasure.

With the print seized on the orders of the Rome public prosecutor, Brando, Schneider, Bertolucci, Grimaldi and their distributor Ubaldo Maltucci were all called to trial in Bologna, but on 2 February, all parties were acquitted and the ban lifted.

Moralists can also be great publicists. The film re-opened 17 February in most of Italy's key cities, and the police had to be called out to control the crowds. But, after quickly becoming one of the most successful films ever released in Italy, an appeal by the proscecution ensued, until finally on 3 February 1976 the High Court of Cassation condemned the film, finding it 'obscene' in its entirety and ordering the confiscation of all extant prints.

It was very bad, because myself, Marlon, Maria and the producer were all condemned to two months of prison with suspension. The negative of the film had to be burned, which was kind of exciting, in the sense of how you can

be excited if you feel you are a martyr – I wanted to set fire to it myself in the
Campo de' Fiori, where the sixteenth-century heretic Giordano Bruno had been
burned in public. Actually, the original negative was I believe safe in France, so
we handed over an internegative. Then I discovered something very frustrating,
which was that I lost my civil rights, so I couldn't vote for five years. The movie
was banned in Italy for fourteen years, until in 1987, by a strange path through
the labyrinth of laws, a judge who liked it was able to free the film again, saying it
was no longer obscene. But I think the young people who saw it after the ban
was lifted were a bit disappointed; they thought it was a very chaste movie. It had
lost the kind of superficial impact while it kept, I think, very much the inner
despair.

In France, the film first opened only in Paris on 15 December 1972, and
after one month had achieved around a million admissions. As *Last Tango*
was banned outright in Franco's Spain, the French border town of
Perpignan did healthy business with a regular influx of sensation-seeking
pilgrims from Barcelona to catch 'the picture that Spain shall not see'.
The film also played for months in Biarritz, where it was estimated that
90 per cent of the audience were Spanish.

Meanwhile, back in Britain the moral watchdogs were on the
prowl. *The Sunday Mirror* had paved the way with their 17 December
headline 'Marlon Brando Shocker', claiming the film – probably unseen
by the reporter in question – contained scenes 'calculated to knock the
bottom out of the back-street porno film-market'. British critics even
ventured to Paris to be ahead of their colleagues. Alexander Walker
protested 'This film must be shown' in a long review in the *Evening
Standard* on 1 January 1973, and told the British public that *Last Tango* 'is
going to change our preconditioned attitudes about the extent that we
want films to reflect our lives. … It will divide audiences in Britain in a
way I think very few of us have been prepared for'.

Hot from the debates over *A Clockwork Orange* and *The Devils*,
the press were keen to suggest that the British Board of Film Censors
was under severe pressure over *Last Tango*, conveniently ignoring that any
such duress might be of their own creation. The current Secretary,

Stephen Murphy, saw the film privately in late December 1972, and then with the whole Board a week later. The Censors' report on *Last Tango*, dated 9 January 1973, included the following statement:

This film is certainly not as pornographic as the publicity in the newspapers would have us believe. The buggery sequence is not very explicit … the sex is shown with great restraint, a little too much in my opinion, as Paul seems to accomplish the most strenuous sexual athletics with his trousers on. It is language rather than visuals which seem to be the only real problem.

In the event, it was the notorious sodomy scene which most concerned the Board, and they proposed a cut of about twenty seconds – approximately thirty feet of film – which encompassed half the shot showing this act from the side, and for continuity reasons in the dialogue, the succeeding brief shot of Paul mounting Jeanne. Both director and producer flew to Britain to protest the cut, and in consideration that removing the second shot would affect the dialogue in the scene ('I'm going to tell you about the family …'), the censored section was reduced to the specific shot of Paul inserting his fingers between Jeanne's

The censored shot

buttocks, about ten seconds of film. At the request of the distributors, this decision was not announced until 16 February.

The film opened on 15 March 1973 at the Prince Charles Cinema in London, where it broke the house records and ran for over a year, accompanied by a successful nationwide release.

Last Tango has now quietly passed into the category of films whose controversies no longer seem so important. In fact by the time the film was released on video in the early 90s, and became visible first on satellite TV and then Channel 4 in 1993, the controversy was over. The BBFC (the 'C' now stands for Classification, though of course they still regularly impose cuts) were even happy to restore those precious missing seconds, thus ensuring the British public need no longer doubt the lubricative potential of butter.

3 First Steps

Last Tango is a film open to all manner of interpretation. One persuasive journalist thought it was about the impossibility of finding a decent apartment in Paris. Most obviously, it is a film in the European 'art house' tradition (which had itself penetrated much of Hollywood by the early 70s), a psychological drama about personal anguish and the impossibility of divorcing the sexual from the emotional in our lives. But then, given Bertolucci's own fondness for psychoanalytic viewpoints, the film can be seen to deal with the most deeply embedded patterns of human behaviour, including those reflected in myth. And just as Godard (among others) was reminding us that cinema is an all-encompassing art form constantly reflecting on its own processes, so *Last Tango* also engages with the personalities of the actors just as much as their fictional characters. This complexity (which today can appear a lost art) has led to a wide range of responses to the film, over and above its obvious sexual effrontery. But let's begin at the beginning.

Last Tango in Paris opens with a title sequence featuring two paintings by Francis Bacon, shown separately against black on either side of the screen, and only briefly together before the first actual shot of the film. The first, positioned on the left, is one panel of a diptych, *Double Portrait of Lucien Freud and Frank Auerbach, 1964*; it shows a man (Freud) in white underclothes on a red divan against yellow and white walls. The second, positioned on the right of the screen, is *Study for Portrait (Isabel Rawsthorne), 1964*; the image is of a woman on a wooden chair, sitting cross-legged and wearing a white top and a brown skirt. These two portraits, in their loneliness and ambiguity, could be parallel figures to Paul and Rosa. At the bottom of the frame of the portrait of the woman, there is the shadow of a rat. A rat of course will turn up on the mattress in the apartment.

The use of Bacon was no afterthought. There was a major Bacon exhibition at the Grand Palais in Paris in October 1971, when Bertolucci was in full pre-production, and to which he made regular visits.

Study for Portrait (Isabel Rawsthorne), 1964 (private collection)

The title sequence

I took Vittorio Storaro to see Bacon's paintings, and Fernando Scarfiotti, and Gitt, the costume designer, and they were all very impressed. Vittorio and Fernando ended up playing a lot with frosted glass, and I remember we did these close-ups of Marlon behind the glass, which were very like Bacon. I would say, today we'll do a Bacon, bring the glass! The exhibition continued long enough for me to show it to Marlon. These men in Bacon were for me the visual model for Marlon's character.

What Bertolucci wanted from his character Paul – and what he felt the middle-aged Brando could portray – was the essence of those tortured people in Bacon's paintings. 'He is like one of those Bacon figures who show on their faces all that is happening in their guts – he has the same devastated plasticity.'[6] Even Bacon's self-portraits of this period (1969–70), in which he wears a light-brown overcoat similar to the one worn by Paul, look remarkably like Brando in the film. *Last Tango*'s first image, of Paul screaming 'Fucking God' against the roar of an overhead Metro train as the camera swoops down on him, is like a fusion of Bacon's aesthetic – a face distorted by inner anguish – and that of Bertolucci, the gestural poetry of a camera movement. And given the blasphemy of Brando's cry, could this be considered Bertolucci's 'screaming anti-Pope'?

Brando himself was surprised by this first camera move. According to the film's Second assistant director, Jean-David Lefebvre, the actor declared, 'I can't believe this. Bernardo is completely crazy. He wants me to play this with my back to the camera.' But Brando followed his director's bidding, apparently adding in the scream himself.[7] Introducing your star in this fashion is already a shock; to have him bellow an obscenity (and one that was then still comparatively new to mainstream cinema) doubles the impact.

The entire opening sequence takes place on the Pont de Bir-Hakeim, which Bertolucci also used in the first scene of *The Conformist*. It crosses the Seine south of the Eiffel Tower in the west of the city, and has two levels, with the Metro trains travelling overhead from the elevated station Bir-Hakeim (the same station where Tom and Jeanne will later meet).

At the time of the filming, I knew Paris well, I had friends there, my French was fluent, and I felt I was more a French director than an Italian one. I had shot *The Conformist* there, and I returned to many of the same locations – the bridge at Passy, the Gare d'Orsay – because I was thinking that the murderer always goes back to the place of the crime! But really it was for me a kind of imaginary collage.

As Paul moves forward towards us, dishevelled and downcast in a long camel-hair coat, behind him appears a figure who slowly comes into focus. It is Jeanne, a bustling, smart little bourgeoise, the embodiment of young chic in her fur-collared and fur-cuffed off-white coat, a very short dress, brown leather boots, and a dark wide-brimmed hat. As she passes Paul she glances back at him, but his gaze has already wandered off in the other direction. Below the bridge is a riot police van and a group of helmeted *flics*. As Jeanne gaily skips along, Paul looks up at an apartment building at the end of the bridge.

By the entrance of the building is the sign 'rue Jules Verne'. This is a fabrication of the art department; it is in fact the rue d'Alboni in Passy. Why the change of name? An invitation to a voyage of discovery, or maybe the site of a fantasy world? One of the main music themes of the film, played on strings, is heard – the first music since the opening credits, and the first in a series of punctuations heralding a decisive moment. There is a large frosted glass and ironwork door, behind which glows a burning orange light. Jeanne checks out a notice on the side, which says 'Apartment for rent', and then decides to visit the bar below in the street.

Inside the bar, we repeatedly see a shot in which the screen is sharply divided, with the dully-lit customer area on the left, and the outer toilet door on the right of the screen, which again is made of frosted glass, lit with a warm orange glow from within. It is like two panels of a diptych. Beyond the toilet entrance is where the phone booth is located – another opaque glass door, behind which is a shadowy figure we take to be Paul. At the sink an old woman scrubs her false teeth, and then noisily slips in her dentures – an unflinching close-up. When she

The opening scenes on the bridge at Passy

The rue Jules Verne, the bar, the apartment

leaves, Jeanne mimics her in the mirror, pouting and puffing up her cheeks as if to say, 'Thank God I'm young!'

Jeanne hears the phone booth door opening, and then we see Paul leaving by the outer toilet door. The dislocation of these shots – there is a jump in space and time, losing the moment when Paul and Jeanne might have looked at each other – reinforces their lack of contact. Jeanne engages with the world, while Paul is lost from it. She phones her mother about the apartment, and as she does, the booth door swings open, revealing one perfect bare leg raised against the wall, again in defiance of the old flesh that surrounds her.

Back at the apartment, the concierge is vague and obstreperous (she is played with demonic insouciance by Darling Legitimus, later to be immortalised as the grandmother in Euzhan Palcy's *Rue Cases Nègres* (*Black Shack Alley*, 1983)). After much prevarication, Jeanne is told she can go up on her own, and since the key is mysteriously missing, a duplicate is found.

Once inside the dark apartment, Jeanne opens the windows and lifts up the shutters to reveal walls of a shabby orange-brown colour, with the lower sections a darker red, looking curiously like a tidemark. Although this colour scheme draws parallels with Bacon's own palette, for Bertolucci's cinematographer Vittorio Storaro it also derived from his discovery of a wintry Paris that was illuminated – in bars, offices, apartments – even at midday.

The natural light was so low that the town was used to having all the artificial lights on. The conflict between these two energies (natural and artificial) gave me the different wavelength or vibration, the different grade of Kelvin that can be represented, the different colour that you can take. So I was starting to understand how it can be important to represent the story in this kind of town. I used the colour of orange. Once again it was the different wavelength or energy that gave me the idea; the high level of that wavelength was giving me the impression that it was about passion. We started to paint that empty apartment orange; we started to use the winter sun, which was very low, during the daytime. The light of the sun gave us very warm tones. And the colour of the artificial light next to the daylight suggested this colour too.[8]

Storaro even called to the set his lab technician from Rome to explain the excess of yellow and orange in the rushes of *Last Tango*.

As the light bursts into the room, we can make out a figure hunched on a radiator by the fireplace. It is Paul. Jeanne registers her shock. He tells her he came in before her. They speak in French and English. She looks around, but he shows little interest. 'Are you an American?' she asks. He doesn't respond, but steps on to the floor and crosses the room.

Paul and Jeanne now play a strange kind of dance with each other. He disappears into the shadows of an adjoining room, toying with the pieces of furniture that surround an object covered in a large dust sheet, not responding to her questions. She blithely takes a leak in the bathroom, while a phone starts ringing. Returning to the living room she answers the phone, but he also picks up an extension, mumbling 'There's no-one here … I don't know'. There is a click, but he keeps the receiver under his chin, and slowly approaches Jeanne, the metallic sound of his breathing on the line highlighted on the soundtrack. An erotic tension is building between them. He lets the receiver drop, and then they come face to face. She asks him if he is taking the apartment. Neither is certain. 'Think fast', he says, moving out of frame.

The first embrace

As Jeanne bends down to pick up her hat, a shadow falls over her, and we hear off-screen a door slam. As Paul approaches her, there is a palpable electricity in the air. Bertolucci's camera movements and the subtle changes in focus have been bringing them together, then breaking them apart, and forcing them together again. He takes her hat from her hands, and casts it aside. He picks her up (Hollywood style?), and carries her across the frame towards the window. She shows no resistance, but clasps his shoulders with the tenderness of a child. Once by the window, they begin to kiss passionately, and he tears her panties off, the ripping sound cutting through their sighs. Clasping him round his neck, she straddles him as he penetrates her. In one long take, the camera keeps its distance, only slowly closing in. After he comes, they tumble to the floor. Paul falls off Jeanne, and she rolls towards us, flashing her pubic hair. She clasps her crotch. He gasps, 'God', now in a very different tone. They are two exhausted bodies in an empty space.

4 Dangerous Moves

The apartment becomes an enclosed, private world that belongs solely to Paul and Jeanne; it exists only in the present tense. Paul has his past, represented by the low-grade hotel (flophouse?) that Rosa has left him to run. Jeanne returns to her suburban family house and central apartment, but she is not tied to them. She has the easy mobility of affluent youth. Tom flits around with his crew to locations that serve his desire to love Jeanne on film; his past and present exists only on celluloid. *Last Tango* is essentially an interior drama, in which the outside world rarely intrudes. The political context so evident in Bertolucci's earlier films is now suppressed. Yet, as the director told a young Marina Warner when she visited the set, if he were to demand that she perform oral sex on him, *that* would be a political act.[9]

Jeanne faces
Tom's crew

Immediately after that fateful encounter, Paul and Jeanne go their separate ways with deceptive nonchalance. Jeanne meets her fiancé Tom at the Gare St Lazare, where he has a film crew in attendance. He has failed to tell her that he is filming their relationship for a TV documentary, and Jeanne is irritated by his presumption. But as he tells her, 'We're in a film. From now on … if I kiss you, that may be for the movie.' Tom explains that the documentary is called 'Portrait of a Girl', and that she is the subject. She reacts by calling him a coward and traitor, but then plays the game by becoming mock-romantic. Tom

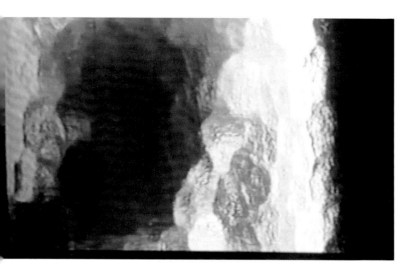

fails to see the irony, and is thrilled with the result. The flippancy of this scene is underlined by the horror of the next, in which a maid (Catherine) is cleaning up a bath covered in blood from the suicide of Rosa. While the music grinds menacingly, and the camera shifts furtively alongside the frosted glass, she appears to be talking to herself, about the questions the police have been asking, and the nature of Rosa's and Paul's relationship.

CATHERINE: The clients awake all night ... the hotel, full of police. ... They playing
around with the blood. All spies! Only questions. If she was sad ... if
she was happy. ... If you fought ... if you hit each other ... and how
long had you been married ... and why you didn't have children ...?
Pigs ...

Suddenly we are aware Paul is standing by the bath. Unlike in the previous scene, in which everyone is bustling about in a loose-limbed parody of *cinéma vérité*, Bertolucci's camera here fragments the elements with close-ups and strong dividing lines within the frame, distorting faces through the glass *à la* Bacon. The red of the blood, the insistent sound of

The Bacon effect

running water, the maid handing over a barber's razor; we are in an abattoir for humans. The parallel with the brutality of Bacon's paintings – flesh cut open, the colour spectrum dominated by red and orange, the isolation of figures in emptied rooms – is obvious.

To add to this physical abstraction, the time scale of the film is difficult to assess. According to the director, 'The story takes place over two or three days but the spectator has the impression that it's a much longer span of time.'[10] This is really a piece of poetic licence, as even taking into account the efficiency of the Paris Metro, by my calculation the events shown would take at least five days. But it's all in keeping with the film's overall sense of dreamy suspension, just as it is hard to say when exactly the lovers meet in the apartment (it always appears to be during daylight).

In the second scene in the apartment, Jeanne arrives alone, and is followed by a parade of removal men with pieces of furniture, including a double mattress. When Paul appears, Jeanne remains casual, suggesting she returned to give him her key. He just gets down to arranging the room. 'What do I care? Take off your coat. Come help me ...' This is the first exchange between them, and it establishes how Paul is to dominate, to set the rules and control the terms of their relationship (traditionally, it is the man who leads in the tango).

'I don't want to know your name'

JEANNe: I don't know what to call you.
PAUL: I don't have a name.
JEANNE: You want to know mine?
PAUL: No! No, I don't – I don't want to know your name. You don't
         have a name, and I don't have a name either. No names here. Not
         one name.

He goes on to tell her, 'You and I are going to meet here without
knowing anything that goes on outside here.' Jeanne accepts the terms,
but in their subsequent meetings persists in trying to find out more about
Paul.

Parallel to their sexual *pas de deux* is interwoven a succession of
scenes involving Tom filming Jeanne, and Paul at his hotel. Rosa's mother
is there to tidy up her dead daughter's possessions and plead for a full
funeral. On the other side of the courtyard, a black saxophonist plays
while a woman repairs his fly with a needle and thread. Throughout the
film, the plangent tone of this instrument will make its mark, and the
raging, near-hysterical quality of Gato Barbieri's solo playing is a perfect
correlative to Brando's cries of anguish and the Bacon-inflected, open-
wound texture of the images. At Bertolucci's request, Barbieri (whose
wife worked on *Before the Revolution*) observed the film at the editing
stage, resulting in music that follows the camera movements; 'it
announces or underlines them according to whether we were seeking
synchronization or conflict.'[11]

I wanted to have Gato Barbieri playing in the film. Because of the tango,
because he's Argentinian, because I love his music, its sound. I knew I would
hear a tenor saxophone, so I put in the script a saxophone being played. I like to
think in secret that *Last Tango* is my version of *An American in Paris*, which is a
musical, and so the music is very important. I wanted a very emotional music
score.

In this scene, the emotion is of a truly pressure-cooker intensity, as Paul
insists there is no clue to the suicide, and (in a violent blow to the door

that caused Brando to injure his hand) he explodes at the suggestion of involving a priest. 'Rosa wasn't a believer. Nobody believes in the fucking God here.' This sequence features the most abstract camera movement in the entire film; when Paul and Rosa's mother first meet face to face, Bertolucci tracks into the door – marked 'Privé' – so as to exclude them both on either side of the frame. There can be no meeting between these characters in this world of darkness and death, just as the occupants of the hotel at the close of the scene cower behind tentatively opened doors, one of which Paul angrily slams shut.

Unlike Paul, Tom wants to know everything about Jeanne. He films her in her suburban family home talking about her childhood, and she recounts memories of her first, apparently innocent love for her cousin, and about her dead father, a colonel who served in Algiers. This figure, in his absent personification of colonial repression, is arguably the one overtly political element in *Last Tango*. She runs from the garden back to the apartment to continue talking about her father, remembering how she admired him in his uniform. But Paul's response is wholly negative: 'All uniforms are bullshit, everything outside this place is bullshit. Besides, I don't want to hear about your stories, about your past and all that.' In spite of this, she goads him into speaking – in one long unbroken take – about his own childhood, but his are largely memories of shame.

She talks about her cousin who was called Paul (a cruel coincidence); he flinches at the name. Although it is Paul who has set the agenda, Jeanne continues to assert her own inner strength, her beauty, her youth, her bourgeois insolence. When she masturbates before him to prove her sexual independence, Paul is left alone with the realisation that his dream of a relationship untainted by history or sentiment is fading fast. As Bertolucci has commented:

I started to make a film about a couple, but instead I made a film about two lonelinesses. … And the scene that is most about this loneliness is the scene in which Maria masturbates and Marlon goes into the other room and cries. He cries because at that moment he is sincere about himself; he sees that he is

Jeanne masturbates, Paul cries, Marcel and Paul in matching robes

The Bacon poses

trying to find in sex a lost innocence – above all, to find through sex an ideal relationship. At that moment, he understands that this is impossible.[12]

It is perhaps the core scene of the film.

In the published screenplay of *Last Tango*, which is a curious amalgam of a shooting script (with extra scenes of little importance no longer in the film) and transcribed improvisations, this scene ends very differently. In the script, there is no masturbation, but the couple are interrupted by a Bible salesman at the door. This sequence was in fact shot with film critic Michel Delahaye playing the visitor, and was included in the film when it was premiered in New York. In her review, Pauline Kael refers to Paul being 'on all fours barking like a crazy man-dog to scare off a Bible salesman who has come to the flat,' and she was upset to discover that Bertolucci had excised the scene. As the director told *The New York Times*: 'Pauline said, "You shouldn't have done this to me," but I never liked that scene. It was meant to be funny, but it was sad, terribly embarrassing somehow. A little too phoney. I've never seen a Bible salesman in Paris; that was just a scriptwriter's perversion.'[13]

The growing inequality in the relationship is amplified in their next encounter. When he tells her, 'I think I'm happy with you,' she becomes delighted and exuberant, and like an indulged child demands more attention, more games from him. For what the relationship thrives on is an adult fantasy of being a child again, free of 'adultness', and all the weight of morality and responsibility that brings. Frustrated by Paul's sudden absence, Jeanne arranges to meet Tom at a Metro station. They shout at each other from opposite platforms, and then as trains clatter pass they break into a wild catfight, which turns into a lovers' embrace.

At night, Paul pays a casual visit on Marcel, a resident of the hotel who he has previously identified as Rosa's lover. They observe that they are wearing identical bathrobes and have the same brand of Bourbon to hand – the legacy of Rosa. Marcel talks about a night when Rosa clawed at the wallpaper in an unprecedented burst of violent rage. Watching Marcel performing his sad exercises to reduce his middle-age spread, Paul wonders what Rosa saw in him – and so really in himself.

When Jeanne next arrives at the apartment, she is greeted by the order, 'Go get the butter'. She finds a hollow square in the floor, but thinks it shouldn't be opened. 'What about that, can I open that?' Paul enquires, patting her stomach. She is not afraid, she says, 'But maybe there's some family secrets inside.' He pins her down on the floor, saying, 'I'll tell you about family secrets.' He pulls back her jeans, applies some butter to her anus, and begins to sodomise her, making her repeat an anti-credo of obscenity and revolt: 'Holy family, the church of good citizens. ... The children are tortured until they tell their first lie. ... Where the will is broken by repression. ... Where freedom is assassinated by egotism.' From this act, ending with his groans and her whimpers, Bertolucci cuts to a Metro train passing by, and then a succession of images of Paul alone in the apartment in a contorted posture, each like a panel in a Bacon triptych. Jeanne sets up her record player, and exacts a petty revenge when she makes Paul plug it in for her and receive an electric shock. He sees her satisfied childlike grin, and says, with some ambiguity, 'You enjoy that?' For him, the act of sodomy appears to be an act of desperate gratification. For her, any pain she has endured seems to be accepted as part of the transgressive fantasy life they share. And vice versa?

Jeanne is next discovered by the Canal St Martin with Tom and his crew. In the spirit of his fictional director's adolescent passion for the cinema, Bertolucci is also paying homage here to the Paris locations of at least two classic 30s French films, Marcel Carné's 1933 *Hotel du Nord* (which was in fact a studio re-creation) and, more significantly, Jean Vigo's *L'Atalante* (1934). In the published screenplay, and from one on-set report, the tribute paid here to Vigo's masterpiece was originally much more explicit. *L'Atalante*, Vigo's only feature before his premature death, concerned the troubled honeymoon of a country girl (Dita Parlo) to a young barge captain (Jean Dasté), whose first mate was memorably played as a raffish old collector of exotic treasures by Michel Simon. Bertolucci first saw *L'Atalante* when he was shooting *Before the Revolution*, and immediately incorporated a homage to it in his film; the future lovers Fabrizio and Gina toss and turn in erotic yearning in their

separate bedrooms just as the estranged couple do in Vigo's magical
love story. In the *Last Tango* screenplay, the scene opens with Jeanne
bargaining over various antiques with the owner of a barge called
'L'Atalante', described as 'an old man with a tattooed chest, identical to
Michel Simon's. Maybe it is he'. In fact the scene was shot with another
Swiss actor, Jean-Luc Bideau.

It was supposed to feature Michel Simon. But at the same time as us, an
American production asked him to do a movie, and he got confused and he
asked something like a million dollars from us for two days, and ten cents from
the Americans for a few weeks!

In what remains of the scene, Tom is on the barge proposing marriage to
Jeanne. Against the white noise of water pouring through the lock, she
half-pretends she can't hear him, mischievously alternating between a

Proposal at the
canal

shouted 'yes' and then 'no'. Frustrated, Tom lifts off the life-saver –
which is inscribed 'L'Atalante' – from around her waist and throws it in
the water. It sinks. Is this a portent of their future together? Or just a
steal from Buster Keaton's *The Boat*? Either way, the romance of an
earlier generation lies at the bottom of the river.

    The following scene finds Jeanne with her mother (played by the
film's costume designer, Gitt Magrini), sorting out the family possessions
in the apartment they share. Jeanne tries on her father's military jacket

and kepi, and plays with his gun, which she says he taught her to use. By wearing his uniform and toying with his weapon, Jeanne not only mocks him but *becomes* him. As she leaves, Jeanne casually informs her mother that she's to be married in a week's time.

Tom has Jeanne on camera again, this time trying on a wedding dress. He interviews her about modern marriage. She says the 'perfect marriage' as formed by the church is no longer possible. The modern marriage – a 'pop' marriage – is like the creation of a car, she continues. If it goes wrong, you have it fixed. Children are a product. But love is something else.

JEANNE: The workers go to a secret apartment. … They take off their overalls, turn back into men and women, and make love.

Sound familiar? As it begins to rain, and the film crew rush for cover, Jeanne runs off to the apartment. Paul arrives and is already in the lift before seeing her. According to Bertolucci, 'When Brando enters the lift, drenched to the bone, and tip taps to let some water out of his shoes, he's my version of Gene Kelly.'[14] Is this American in Paris, who already

Jeanne 'becomes' her father

brings with him the heavyweight aura of a Hemingway or a Miller, the same would-be artist on the G.I. Bill who Minnelli gave us in 1951, now grown into full middle-age and living in a less optimistic age? Jeanne joins him in the lift, mischievously lifting her skirt as they ascend. But though she is horny for him again, she hints that the nature of their liaison may be changing. 'Forgive me! I wanted to leave you and I couldn't. I can't. Do you still want me?' She screams when she sees a dead rat on the bed; Paul picks it up and mocks her by suggesting he serve it up for dinner. Now she is disgusted with him again. 'I can't take it any more here. I'm going away. I'm never coming back, never.'

But in the next shot, he is soaping her in the bath. She taunts him about his age, and indeed Paul washes her with a distinctly paternal affection. She tells him she has fallen in love with a man. He mocks her for dreaming about marital dependency to escape her own loneliness.

JEANNE: But I've found this man.
PAUL: No, you're alone. You're all alone. And you won't be able to be free of that feeling of being alone until you look death right in the face. I mean, that sounds like bullshit and some romantic crap. Until you go right up into the ass of death – right up his ass – till you find a womb of fear. And then, maybe, maybe then you can – you'll be able to find him.
JEANNE: But I've found this man. He's you. You're that man!

This proves to be the pivotal moment in the film. His reaction is to have Jeanne enact the metaphor for real, ordering her to cut her nails and then sodomise him with her fingers – 'right up my ass'. As she performs his request, he calls upon her to agree to have sex with a pig, and then to swallow the pig's vomit and smell its dying farts. Jeanne agrees to follow his example, and promises to do 'more than that. And worse. Worse than before'. It is another assault on the norm of the bourgeois family, only this time he sacrifices his own virility to be penetrated himself.

This is the last time we see Paul and Jeanne together in the apartment. In the following scene, Paul faces his dead wife lying surrounded by an excess of flowers on a bed in the hotel – looking 'death

in the face'. In a monologue in which he expresses his grief and disgust with equal ferocity, he insults her in the vilest terms he can summon up and weeps at his incomprehension of her suicide.

PAUL: Even if the husband lives 200 fucking years, he's never going to be able to discover his true wife's nature. I mean, I might be able to comprehend the universe, but I'll never discover the truth about you, never.

It is an actor's *tour de force*, which if it were not for the consistency of Brando's performance throughout would probably crush the rest of the film. With his long, unrelenting takes, Bertolucci puts the audience in that sickly-sweet smelling room with the actor and his private (real?) agonies, and the experience of watching is as disturbing as it is cathartic.

Paul is distracted from his monologue by an old whore demanding a room at the hotel. When her client sheepishly runs off, she persuades Paul to pursue him. Finding him in an alley, he perfunctorily beats him up, and then lets him go. Appalled by this perverse act of duty, he returns to be alone in his room.

Jeanne now finds the apartment empty, with no evidence of Paul anywhere. Angrily, she pulls down the dust sheet in the side room where he has often retreated, but there is nothing significant underneath, just

'Right up my ass'

more old furniture. The mystery is over, the excitement the apartment brought to her has ended. The concierge once again is no help. Jeanne calls Tom over to see the apartment (her original reason for viewing it), but he finds it smelly and depressing. They agree to look elsewhere to begin their adult life. His film, he announces, is over, and he didn't accomplish anything.

But while Tom's film is over, is that true for the one we have been watching starring Paul?

Paul faces the dead Rosa

5 Full Circle

With Jeanne abandoning the apartment, the final act of the film begins. As she walks across the bridge (in the opposite direction from the very first scene of the film), Paul suddenly appears beside her, now dressed more casually in a jacket and tie. With the loss of Rosa now behind him,

Back on the bridge

'The tango is a rite'

his demeanour is quite changed – he smiles, he jokes. Jeanne, however, is impatient with him.

PAUL: It's me again.
JEANNE: It's over.
PAUL: Yes, it's over. Then it begins again.
JEANNE: What begins again? I don't understand anything anymore.
PAUL: Well, there's nothing to understand. We left the apartment, and now we begin again with love and all the rest of it.

Paul has allowed to happen what he once forbade himself. He wanted a relationship that only existed in the present, and did so by denying the past. Now he wants to believe in a future. He begins to spill out who he is, claiming that despite his age 'I'm still a good stick man even if I can't have any children'.

Crashing the competition

The couple arrive at a dance hall where a tango competition is in progress. 'You know the tango is a rite,' says Paul to Jeanne as they watch the determined competitors strut their stuff. 'But this place is so pitiful,' Jeanne comments. She is right. The dancers look like newly polished waxworks or life-size dolls, and their movements are stiff and mechanical. The tango is drained of its sexual charge, for despite the extreme closeness of the partners, they appear glued rather than magnetised, and Bertolucci's low camera angles underline their absurdity. How sterile life is, outside the apartment. When Paul and Jeanne crash the competiton, their drunken, improvised swirling earns the wrath of the president of the jury, to whom Paul bares his arse (a favourite Brando party trick). When he protests that 'It's love,' she replies, 'But it's a contest. Where does love fit in? Go to the movies to see love!'

But shouldn't this dance be the ultimate dance of passion between two people? Traditionally of course, the tango originated in the brothels of Buenos Aires, a blending of African tribal rhythms from the slaves and the popular Spanish and Italian song traditions of the European immigrants. It became famous in the 1920s through the records of

Carlos Gardel and Valentino's dancing in *The Four Horsemen of the Apocalypse* (1921), and then again in recent decades thanks to the late bandoneon player and composer, Astor Piazzola (in fact, originally Bertolucci wanted Piazzola to collaborate with Barbieri on the score).

Returning drunkenly to their table, Jeanne masturbates Paul in a mechanical fashion under the table, and then beats a retreat. Paul rushes after her into the streets, and with occasional pauses for breath, follows her into her family apartment, chasing up the stairs as she ascends in the lift. He finally faces her in the apartment, and dons her father's cap.

PAUL: This is the title shot, baby. We're going all the way. It's a little old, but full of memory now. How do you like your hero? Over easy or sunny side up? You ran through Africa and Asia and Indonesia. Now I've found you. And I love you. I want to know your name.

He has failed to notice she is holding her father's revolver. As she speaks her name – 'Jeanne' – the gun goes off.

Paul dons the kepi

'I don't know his name'

Paul staggers to the balcony. He mumbles a series of broken thoughts. 'Our children. Our children. Our children. Will remember ...' He looks out over the city, takes out his chewing gum and sticks it under the railing. We stare out at the Paris skyline just as Paul did, and then the camera tilts down to reveal him lying in a foetal position on the balcony floor. It tracks back to show Jeanne to the left of frame, looking away from him into space, intoning a statement for the police.

JEANNE: I don't know who he is. He followed me on the street. He tried to rape me. He's a madman. I don't know his name. I don't know his name. I don't know who he is ...

She repeats these lines, but is drowned out by a crescendo of music on the soundtrack. The screen cuts to black as the music ends abruptly.

Is this a satisfying end to the film? The first time I saw *Last Tango*, I was disappointed by the melodramatic tidiness of the conclusion. I felt the introduction of a gun (which in true Chekovian fashion, Jeanne plays with earlier on) reduced the film, made it more conventional where before it had broken aggressively free from such dramatic devices. But considering Bertolucci's disparate inspirations, the last scene follows both a tradition of Hollywood melodrama – for example, Vincente Minnelli's *Some Came Running* (1958) – and even more the early pseudo-thrillers of the *nouvelle vague*, for whom it was a recurrent device, Godard's *A bout de souffle* (*Breathless*, 1959) being the obvious example. *Last Tango* echoes *A bout de souffle* in its juxtaposition of France and the USA (Belmondo mimics Bogart, Seberg *is* an American in Paris) and in the way the woman stands at the end, complicit in the death of her lover. There is also the Romantic tradition that we should be destroyed by what we love, or destroy it ourselves. Paul himself breaks the fantasy of his relationship with Jeanne, and he pays the price.

In his convoluted study of Bertolucci's cinema, *Bertolucci's Dream Loom: A Psychoanalytic Study of Cinema*, T. Jefferson Kline offers up a number of mythical readings of Bertolucci's films, and *Last Tango* is no exception. He relates the story to the Orpheus legend, in which the poet musician, inconsolable at the death of his wife Eurydice, gains entrance to Hades and is allowed to take her out of the Underworld on the condition that he should not turn back to look at her as they leave. He of course cannot resist doing so, and loses her forever. In *Last Tango*, Paul and Jeanne cross the bridge over the Seine to reach the apartment, just as in the myths it was necessary to cross the Styx to reach Hades. The apartment building is guarded by a sinister concierge – the Eumenides, perhaps – and in the street there is a group of riot police, echoing the uniformed riders who were the guardians of Death in Jean Cocteau's *Orphée* (1950), an interpretation of the myth that was well known to Bertolucci (and to which he later paid homage by his casting of its lead actor, Jean Marais, in *Stealing Beauty*). When the lovers meet outside the apartment, Jeanne declares 'It's over,' but Paul violates his own rule – Orpheus' disobedience – as they recross the bridge, condemning himself to death just as he discovers her name (is it by chance that Brando once played an Orpheus surrogate in Sidney Lumet's *The Fugitive Kind* (1960), based on the Tennessee Williams play *Orpheus Descending?*).

If the parallel is to be accepted, then it is also true that Bertolucci's deployment of the myth is a complex and perverse one. Key to this is the concept of the double, for then, according to Kline, 'the erotic-aggressive ambivalence expressed towards Jeanne can thus be understood as a displacement of Paul's frustrations and anger at Rosa. Bertolucci uses the Orpheus myth to explore many of the deeper implications of Paul's attempt at recuperation or psychic recovery of his wife/mother figure.'

It is obvious to even a casual viewer of *Last Tango* that Bertolucci incorporates a web of doublings and mirror images in his story. This trope was particularly explicit in *Partner* (based on Dostoevsky's *The Double*) in which Pierre Clementi played a split personality, and again in *The Spider's Stratagem* in which father and son were portrayed by the same actor. Later, in *Novecento*, he would construct the whole story from the lives of two men born on the same day, one an aristocrat and the other a peasant on his estate.

So in *Last Tango*, Paul loses his wife Rosa, and if Jeanne and Tom are to have children, he wants to call their daughter Rosa; Jeanne's first love was her cousin called Paul, who she tells her new love Paul about before re-enacting her adolescent masturbation game; Jeanne lost her father during the Algerian war, and Paul is old enough to be her father, and dons his kepi in the final scene; Rosa had a husband in Paul and a lover in Marcel, and had them both wear the same bathrobe and keep the same Bourbon to hand (there is even an extra doubling here in the casting of Marcel; he is Massimo Girotti, who played a similar kind of role to Brando in the Italian cinema of the 40s and 50s, most notably in Visconti's *Ossessione* (1942)). As laid out for her funeral, Rosa appears to be wearing a wedding dress like the one Jeanne wore in the preceding scene. Then there is a more ambiguous association – and here lies perhaps the clue to Kline's interpretation of the film – when Paul bites Rosa's mother on the hand (the act of a frustrated child) and teasingly comments that Rosa and her mother were very alike.

PAUL: Rosa was a lot like you. People must have told you often. ... Isn't that right, Mother?

MOTHER: Up until ten years ago they were still saying it – two sisters ...

Remember too that Paul has effectively been kept by Rosa, as she is still regarded as the owner of the hotel. When he acts as pimp to the ageing whore, perhaps he is replaying his role with Rosa, and this painted apparition at his door is a terrible image of what Rosa herself might have become. Paul's face at the window actually replaces the reflection of the whore's reluctant client, and so when he beats the man up, he is also expressing his self-hatred by attacking a mirror image.

Until the moment he confronts Jeanne outside the apartment, Paul is failing to resolve the death of Rosa, which he sees as an act of betrayal: 'You're worse than the dirtiest street pig that anybody could ever find anywhere, and you know why? Because you lied. You lied to me and I trusted you.' The sexual trysts with Jeanne are a form of renewal for him, an act of regeneration that he refuses to recognise for

what it is. When he tells Jeanne that she can only find a man to love her when she has entered the 'womb of fear', he is actually describing the womb-like apartment; not only do we almost hear 'room' in that sentence, but the very texture of the apartment is, as was admitted by the set designer, 'all uterine'. The room becomes an adult playpen, where Jeanne can feel like a child again and Paul can cover up his psychic scars.

But in fact, as Jeanne becomes an adult in the act of killing Paul, so he regresses into a child. His strange utterances, 'Our children … will remember,' following an earlier declaration that he can't have children, are dramatically confusing and have led to a lot of head-scratching. Perhaps he is just commenting on a generation beyond the troubles they have had to endure. As he stares out over Paris, he takes his chewing gum and places it under the railing. He then mumbles something in a strange language. Brando improvised this, not initially revealing to the director what it meant other than to say it was in Tahitian. According to Bertolucci, he finally told him it was the name of his island, Tetiaroa, though the director reminds us that Brando likes to play games and this may be true or false. Perhaps in these two cryptic gestures the actor Marlon Brando is simply taking off his mask, and preparing to go home

Paul shadowed by the whore's client

(the film was mainly shot in chronological order). The next image we see of him, he is crumpled on the floor of the balcony in a foetal position. The regression is complete.

Kline also offers this thought on *Last Tango*: 'Through the voyage enacted in this film, we may better understand the degree to which cinema itself is an Orphic experience: to descend into the darkness of a protracted space in an effort to retrieve through images a lost origin.' When we go to the movies, don't we also enter a secret room to enjoy a fantasy life without a past or a future?

6 Marlon/Paul

I love Marlon Brando in the movies, but when I see *Last Tango* I think it is one of his best, most convincing roles – no masks, no Actors Studio mannerisms.

By the time he made *Last Tango*, Brando's image had gone through many changes, but essentially he remained the man who defined screen acting for the generation that followed, from Newman to Penn via Nicholson, De Niro and Pacino. To begin with, he was the dedicated 'method' actor who spent a long period in a wheelchair before making his movie début as a crippled soldier in Fred Zinnemann's *The Men* (1950). Subsequently he transposed his animalistic, searingly intense Stanley Kowalski in Tennessee Williams' *A Streetcar Named Desire* (1951) from the Broadway stage to screen under Elia Kazan's direction. But while a few memorable roles followed, especially with Kazan at the helm – *Viva Zapata!* (1952) and *On the Waterfront* (1954) – he fell victim to the Hollywood machine by taking on unsuitable character parts. However, the one image he could never quite shake off was that of the leather encrusted biker in *The Wild One* (1954), flexing his macho attitude. 'Hey Johnny, what are you rebelling against?', was the taunting question. 'Waddya got?', came the smart answer. And if the film itself was no revolutionary tract, it made the actor an icon of youthful rebellion.

But unlike James Dean, Brando didn't 'live fast, die young, leave a good looking corpse'. He grew older (and fatter), as did his disillusionment with acting and the cinema, so he became instead a rebel with a cause. He marched with Martin Luther King, and he became a spokesman for the Native American, fighting alongside them for fishing rights in the state of Washington. Many of his 60s movies were done just for the paycheck, while in-between times he would live in splendid isolation on Tetiaroa, the island he bought near Tahiti. But 1972 became a pivotal year for Brando thanks to two films: *The Godfather* and *Last Tango in Paris*.

Marlon Brando was born in 1924 in Omaha, Nebraska. His family – two sisters, a proud, cultured mother and a domineering father – were

A Streetcar Named Desire

The Wild One

of old Midwest stock and enjoyed middle-class comforts. Marlon Brando Snr was a salesman and then a sales executive, a job that entailed him travelling a great deal, during which time he began extramarital affairs. His wife, Dorothy or 'Dodie', diverted herself with the arts and especially local theatre, but also became increasingly alcoholic. With the Depression, the family eventually relocated in 1938 to a farmhouse on an eight-acre property in Libertyville, Illinois. The young Marlon – known as 'Bud' – enjoyed a rural childhood surrounded by farm animals (including a Guernsey cow named Betsy), and this would be exactly – and painfully – recalled in *Last Tango*, when Jeanne provokes Paul to talk about his youth, and Brando supplied the following improvisation:

PAUL: My father was a … a drunk, whore-fucker, bar-fighter, super-masculine, and he was tough. … My mother was … very poetic, also drunk, and my memories 'bout when I was a kid was of her being arrested nude. We lived in a small town. Farming community. We lived on a farm. Well, I'd come home after school and and she's be gone on a – in jail or something. I used to have to milk a cow. Every morning and every night. And I liked that, but I remember one time I was all dressed up to go out and take this girl to a basketball game. And I started to go out and my father said, 'You have to milk the cow.' And I asked him, 'Would you please milk it for me?' And he said, 'No, get your ass out there!' So I went out, and I was in a hurry and didn't have time to change my shoes, and I had cowshit all over my shoes, and on the way to the basketball game it smelled in the car. … Just. … I – I can't remember very many good things.

In his autobiography, *Songs My Mother Taught Me*, Brando confessed to the accuracy of these recollections. Some of the memories in this improvisation are of happier times: he talks of the family house, how his mother taught him to love nature, and his fondness for his black Great Dane called Dutchie. He recalls a farmer from the time he worked in a ditch draining land, and how he never could see the spit fall off the bowl of his pipe – this related to his enforced work detail in the summer of

1943, following his expulsion from the Shattuck Military Academy in Faribault.

Not all the Brando biography in *Last Tango* is spoken directly by the actor himself. When the maid Catherine is cleaning up the bloody aftermath of Rosa's suicide, in recounting her conversation with the police, she gives us a potted history of the Brando character.

CATHERINE: They said, 'Nervous type, your boss? You know he was a boxer?' So? 'That didn't work ... so he became an actor, then a racketeer on the waterfront in New York.' So? 'It didn't last long ... played the bongo drums ... revolutionary in South America ... journalist in Japan. ... One day he lands in Tahiti, hangs around, learns some French ... comes to Paris and then meets a young woman with money ... he marries her ... and since then ... what does he do now, your boss. Nothing.'

What is given here is a distorted résumé of Brando's screen roles, as if murkily glimpsed through one of the film's frosted panes of glass: Terry Molloy, the failed boxer turned dockworker in *On the Waterfront*; Emiliano Zapata, the Mexican revolutionary in *Viva Zapata!*; Harrison Carter MacWhite, the journalist in *The Ugly American*, combined with Major Lloyd Gruver in Japan in *Sayonara*; Fletcher Christian in *Mutiny On the Bounty*, during the making of which Brando fell in love with Tahiti; and finally, Paul in *Last Tango in Paris*. Plus his genuine skill as a player of bongo drums, and the fact that his broken nose emanated from an impromptu boxing match during the stage run of *A Streetcar Named Desire*. In 1976, Brando told *Rolling Stone* magazine that '[Bertolucci] had some cockamamie notion. What he wanted to do was sort of meld the image of the actor, the performer, with the part. So he got a few extraneous details. Played the drums, I don't know ... Tahiti ... so that the man is really telling the story of his life. I don't know what the hell it's supposed to mean.'[15]

Even before he made *Last Tango*, Bertolucci had said, 'All my films are documentaries on my actors. I follow them. I let them do what they want.'[16] But this was a film in which he actively encouraged this from the outset. The haunting elisions between Brando's own personality and the character in *Last Tango* had evolved from the first encounters between Bertolucci and Brando, when they shared details of their personal lives. As Bertolucci said to *The New York Times*, 'It was a great synchronization. I wanted him to forget Paul and remember himself and what was inside him. For him it was a completely new method. He was fascinated by the risk, and afraid of the sense of violation of his privacy.'[17]

We started with Jean-Pierre Léaud a week before Marlon arrived, but on the first day of shooting with Brando, after the first take, the camera operator said, 'We must redo it, because I looked through the viewfinder and saw Marlon Brando, and I stopped moving, I was so astonished!' This was in fact the first shot of the film, where he screams 'Fucking God'. Then Vittorio looked at me and said, 'Listen, there is a problem. Marlon's too red.' He had brought along his own make-up. So I said to Marlon, 'Vittorio thinks your make-up's too much for the camera.' He said, 'Oh yes', and went off to his caravan, and took a towel to his face, which then became very red. He said. 'How's that?' And we said, 'That's perfect'. We had heard that the same thing had happened on *Mutiny On the Bounty*, when in the first scene he was surrounded by a thousand extras, but he had insisted that if it didn't work for him, then they would have to change the make-up of all the extras.

At the time, Bertolucci confessed to his apprehension in directing Brando.

When I saw him do his first sequence, looking up at the train and crying out, I was shocked. He started at such a violent pitch that I said to myself, 'Maybe I cannot work at the level of this actor'. I was very scared. My fear lasted for the first week, and then Marlon made me understand that he had the same feeling about me. From that moment on, everything worked very well.[18]

The director and his star would often huddle together to discuss their private feelings, sharing their common experience of undergoing extensive analysis.

(Overleaf) The lovers entwined

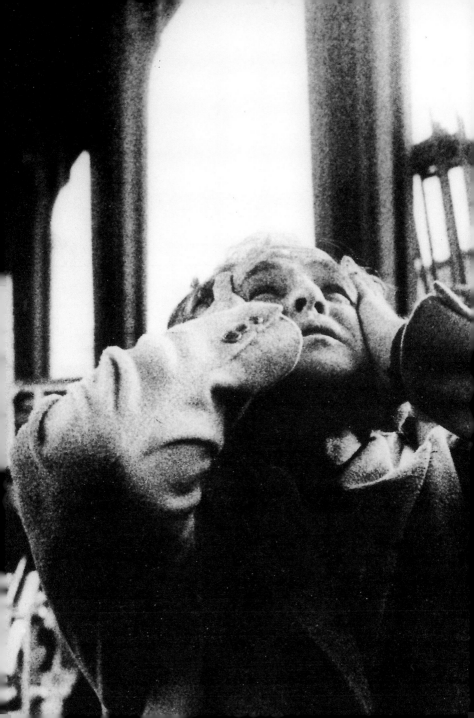

I was in my second or third year of analysis and I was very excited about it, and I thought it could be a fantastic way to reach very secret places in the mind and the soul of the actors. So I was using it to stimulate and provoke. It was a kind of a little triggering of things. It's not that I decided to have a method, it was just a way of approaching things, of reading between the lines, of looking behind the mask.

Marlon was really one of the easiest actors I've worked with, he would never ask embarrassing questions about the reason why I was telling him to do something. The only thing is he wouldn't shoot on Saturday, but we had to go on shooting on Saturdays because we were on location. So every Saturday he would send cocktails and canapés to the crew – all very pleasant.

In his autobiography, Brando asserts that 'Bernardo wanted me to make love to Maria Schneider to give the picture more authenticity. But it would have completely changed the picture and made our sex organs the focus of the story, and I refused.' But Bertolucci disputes this.

It's not true that I wanted real penetration. I wouldn't have wanted to do that to Maria. There was a scene of Marlon doing frontal nudity, but I cut it for reasons of structure.

The fact that Brando remains clothed in most of the intimate scenes only emphasises the age difference between him and Schneider. By Schneider's account, though she felt free to be naked in the film, for Brando it was definitely a problem. 'I wasn't excited by him, although my friends told me I should be, and I don't think he was excited by me. He's old, almost fifty, you know, and he's flabby and he has a big … [she gestures to indicate a pot belly]. And he was very uptight about it.'[19] Brando may have agonised about his weight but apparently at the director's insistence – he does play one scene totally naked, with Schneider's limbs entwining him in such a way as to obscure any excess flab. As to revealing his genitals on camera, in his autobiography Brando recalls that the attempt to do just that in one scene failed to work because 'It was such a cold day that my penis shrank to the size of a peanut'. And as Bertolucci comments:

(Previous) Preparing the first shot

After what he has said about his state, I think it should have been peanut butter! Actually, the idea of the butter came when we were having breakfast with Marlon and discussing the scene for that day, which was the buggery scene. There was the usual basket of baguettes with some butter, and I think it was Marlon who made the suggestion. I thought immediately of Bataille's *The Story of the Eye,* in which there is very important use of eggs. I was thinking, butter, eggs, same family!

Brando was to contribute enormously to the language of the film, and the slang he uses is very much that of his generation. In his final pursuit of Jeanne, Paul explains that 'I come from a time when a guy like me would drop into a joint like this and pick up a young chick like you and call her a bimbo'. This brings an authenticity to the scripted scenes that the Italian writers could never have approached. But a combination of laziness and a search for spontaneity had led the actor to ask for a safety net when it came to performance. As Schneider observed, 'Sometimes he didn't want to learn his lines, and he'd put them on cue cards around the room, and he'd fix it so the camera angle would always be right so he could read the lines. The cue cards were right behind the camera! One scene, when he rolled his eyes and looked up very dramatically, he was really looking up to read his lines.'[20] A popular story circulated that on one occasion it had even been necessary to write Brando's lines on Schneider's buttocks. According to Bertolucci, there were certainly a series of practical jokes being played on the actor by the cast and crew, including writing his cues on Schneider's forehead when she was feeding him lines off-camera.

The period of filming *Last Tango* was not a particularly calm one in terms of the actor's private life. His personal finances were in disarray. After he left the USA for Paris, Anna Kashfi, his former wife, took their son Christian to Mexico, and Brando, interpreting this as a kidnapping, had his lawyers demand full custody of the teenage boy. Brando had to return to Los Angeles to appear in court; officially, he was given a week off to attend the New York premiere of *The Godfather* on 14 March. In court on 13 March, Brando was given permission to take his son to Paris for the remainder of the *Last Tango* shoot, and returned to France a relieved man.

At the same time, the response to *The Godfather* (which opened in the USA in 1972) was overwhelming. Brando's reputation was restored – at least until he refused his Oscar the following year, and made it a platform for his support of the Native American. He was subsequently nominated (along with Bertolucci) for *Last Tango*, but controversial European-based films with scenes of sodomy do not as a rule win Academy Awards.

7 Maria/Jeanne

I find it hard to resist Pauline Kael's assessment of Bertolucci's final choice for Jeanne.

Maria Schneider's freshness – Jeanne's ingenuous corrupt innocence – gives the film a special radiance. When she lifts her wedding dress to her waist, smiling coquettishly as she exposes her pubic hair, she's in a great film tradition of irrepressibly naughty girls. She has a movie face – open to the camera, yet no more concerned about it than a plant or a kitten.

Kael also picked up on Bertolucci's inspiration for this character: 'Jeanne is like the adorably sensual bitch-heroines of French films in the twenties and thirties – both shallow and wise.'[21] Her predecessors might be Janie Marèze in *La Chienne* (1931) or Simone Simon in *La Bête humaine* (1938), both directed by Jean Renoir. The director agrees. 'Physically she is reminiscent of a typical French woman, like those painted by Renoir father and son; those women who can walk serenely all over the corpses of the men who fall in love with them.'[22]

Though the film-maker or critic may make such associations, the impression given by Jeanne in the film – closely mirrored by Schneider herself in the interviews she gave at the time – is that she exists only for herself, rejecting traditions, living for the moment. Of course, Jeanne's youth and her bourgeois origins mean that the banalities and irritations of material life don't trouble her. Bertolucci supplies us with very few details of her everyday existence, at least in his final cut. On-set reports and press hand-outs suggest that there were originally more scenes involving Jeanne and her friends, the red-headed twins who appear in the dress shop, charging about in 'their shop truck through many of the city's busy streets and boulevards'. Some reviewers talked about Jeanne being an antiques dealer, though there is little evidence for this in the finished film. As it stands, Jeanne's chic clothes and her swishingly confident stride are more expressive of her than anything she does – like many a young beauty, she just has to *be*. The

Tom makes Jeanne his star

wearying aspects of becoming an adult have yet to impinge on her pleasure in life.

In the published screenplay, there are additional lines of dialogue in the early scenes between Paul and Jeanne that suggest a more romantically cloudy, more gullible character than the one Schneider incarnates. And more easily embarrassed too. In place of a long exchange sparked by her outrage at Paul barging in on her in the bathroom, we have the charged silence of Jeanne entering the apartment

to find Paul already there, and both of them casually removing their shoes preparing for sex. Shame and fear are not part of this Jeanne's make-up. In the bathroom scene where she is completely naked, standing beside Paul as he shaves himself with an old-fashioned blade razor (the same one that was the instrument of Rosa's death?), the juxtaposition of her exposed, smooth young flesh and the sharp metal may put the audience on edge, but not Jeanne nor the actress who plays her.

Unlike Paul, who draws deep pain from his recollections of childhood, Jeanne's memories are so recent as to be a series of games and make-believe. Her sexual past consists of masturbation contests. And her protected, comfortable bourgeois upbringing – a pet dog and an attentive nurse who kept the Arabs away in Algeria, a large country house

– remains for her an idyll. As she tells Tom, her childhood was running wild in the garden, and she believes 'Growing old is a crime'.

In the apartment, Jeanne tells Paul, 'It's like playing grown-ups when you're little. I feel like a child again here.' Paul is also of course both a lover and a father figure to her. When Paul pleases her, she wants the pleasure to go on and on – for children have no sense of proportion, never wish to be told you cannot go further. An adult relationship would involve compromise, balance, responsibility. When Jeanne talks to Tom of marriage, she mocks the conventions and cynically describes it like a product being advertised. If these interviews reveal a different, smarter Jeanne to the one encountered in the apartment, it must be recorded that they were in fact penned by another hand.

The dialogue for the interviews was actually written by Alberto Moravia. Moravia in the 60s had done some beautiful interviews with Stefania Sandrelli and Claudia Cardinale, so I went to him and said I would like him to write just these interviews for the film. We were friends, and he said, 'Why not?' So there were to be one, two, three, one about marriage, one about love, and so on. I just gave him the bare details, she was a young middle-class girl with a boyfriend who is interviewing her, that's all. And I remember very well going twice to see him after lunch, and Moravia was saying, 'What's it about?' And I said, 'Getting married, what it means today in modern life.' He'd think for about fifteen seconds, and then would open his pen and start to write. He would never take his pen away from the page, it would flow from his brain, through his arm, through his fountain pen to the page. He didn't want it to be known that he wrote these dialogues, because he didn't want to pay the taxes! Now, fortunately, I can reveal this fact.

Some commentators have seen Jeanne as just a submissive, foolish young woman willing to be brutalised by Paul in a typical male sadomasochistic fantasy. But the nature of their relationship is more complex and open. As Molly Haskell noted in *From Reverence to Rape*:

Bertolucci brings together the necessary and sometimes contradictory elements in eroticism for women. For if he is saying that the 'sex-only' affair is doomed, he suggests that it is also necessary. In surrendering her body 'without strings', without receiving any assurances of emotional involvement, without making any claims for the spirit, she has a better chance of freeing her mind from its enslavement to the body (whether from over- or under-evaluation), and of freeing herself from that emotional dependency, the compulsion to suffering, that is so often a product of fear rather than freedom. Schneider's journey under Brando's instructions into her own entrails is a terrifying one, but if she emerges she will be in such possession of herself that she won't have to hold on for dear life anymore.

With each encounter between Paul and Jeanne, Paul ensures – usually with a direct question – that she is acquiescent in his desires before he acts on them. Although some saw the first fuck as closer to rape, it is in fact clear from Jeanne's body language that she is an equal partner. It is Tom – her worshipper – who attacks her physically on the Metro station platform. If there is an aggressor in the film, it is him (and his camera), and she demands that he find someone else for his documentary, 'Because you're taking advantage of me, because you force me to do things I've never done before. ... I'm tired of being raped'.

Schneider was happy with the film at the time of its release. 'People are sick who say this film is pornographic,' she told *The New York Times*. 'Nudity for me is beautiful and natural, and the film is full of alive and natural things. It is a film about loneliness and anguish more than it is about sex.'[23] She was unconcerned about Brando's reluctance to appear nude with her, but she was troubled by how willing her character was to submit to Paul's demands. 'I am not at all submissive, and that bothered me. At first I thought, "Bertolucci, you hate women". But I no longer think the film is a put-down of women. Because at the end, after Paul says they'll marry and have children, Jeanne makes the final decision and she rejects him.'[24]

Why did Bertolucci cast this unknown? According to Schneider, the director was impressed 'because I had the body of a man and a woman. You know, big breasts and very skinny from the waist down.'[25] This ambiguity may have been an influence on one famous viewer of the film. In an interview with *Oui* magazine, the Swedish director Ingmar Bergman declared that *Last Tango* was really a film about two homosexuals. 'If you think about it in those terms, [the film] becomes very, very interesting. Except for her breasts, that girl, Maria Schneider, is just like a young boy. There is much hatred of women in this film, but if

Schneider on set with Bertolucci

you see it as being about a man who loves a boy, you can understand it.
It all makes sense this way.' Bergman felt that Bertolucci and Brando had
probably even initially had this idea themselves. 'It would have been very
courageous if they had made it with a boy. As it is now, it makes no sense
as a film.' When *Variety* sought out Bertolucci for a response to this, he
retorted that although he was happy to accept 'all interpretations of my
film', he had never seen the story in these terms. 'Maybe it's a projection
of Bergman's own troubles, his own problems.'[26]

Maria was great and wild. Unfortunately, with all the success she had with the
movie, it was kind of a shock for her. She didn't have the cultural background of
books and knowledge to filter that ferocious success she had, and all at the age
of twenty. Also she fell into the trap of talking too much. She went to New York
and she had one page of *The New York Times* all to herself, a long interview in
which she said she had slept with fifty men and twenty women – wild stuff, it was
the long wave of 1968 going on.

'I'm bisexual completely', Schneider told *The New York Times*. 'I'm
incapable of fidelity: I have need for a million experiences. Women I love
more for beauty than for sex. Men I love for grace and intelligence.'[27]
On the subject of drugs she was equally outspoken; she had tried heroin
and cocaine, but her preference was for pot. In the absence of Brando
(United Artists tried to bribe him into giving interviews with the gift of a
custom-built Rolls Royce, but it was no dice), the young Maria faced a
series of reporters who lapped up her rash outspokenness. She was the
illegitimate daughter of French star Daniel Gelin (curiously enough, an
old friend of Brando's from his first trip to Paris in 1949), but was raised
by her Romanian-born mother Marie-Christine Schneider, who ran a
bookstore in Paris. At fifteen she landed herself the stage role of a
dancer in a French comedy, *Superposition*. This led to a few very minor
film roles, and then a lead part as a young existentialist in Roger Vadim's
low-budget semi-autobiographical drama set in 1952, *Hellé* (1973),
which was released after *Last Tango*. She spent four days at the Actors
Studio in Paris, but gave it up: 'It was not real. It was all technique.

I feel that is damaging to acting. You learn about acting by acting, and in life.'[28]

Schneider's career was not to fulfil this early promise. She was an elusive presence opposite Jack Nicholson in Antonioni's *The Passenger* (aka *Profession: Reporter*, 1975), a film in which there was barely any sex or nudity. But whenever the press came near her, she complained that all they wanted to talk about was the butter scene in *Last Tango*. She then clashed with Luis Buñuel on the set of *That Obscure Object of Desire* (1977) and was fired after four days shooting, leading the Spanish master to revert to his earlier thoughts on her role and divide it between two actresses.

Schneider was due to be reunited with Bertolucci on *Novecento* (1976), playing Anita, the revolutionary schoolteacher, alongside Dominique Sanda, the original Jeanne. But according to Bertolucci, 'She came to Parma for three days and already she was different. "I will not do a scene in the nude," she said. "But there isn't one," I pointed out. She left rather dramatically. A phone call to my hotel – "Maybe I shouldn't be in your film," she said. "Maybe you're right," I said. And she was gone.'[29] Schneider was replaced by Stefania Sandrelli. Having lost her position as the darling of early 70s art cinema, the roles offered to her became less significant and interesting. As far as the press were concerned, the scandals surrounding her drug habits, occasional hospitalisation and public lesbianism took over from the on-screen work. During the filming in Rome of René Clément's *The Babysitter* (1975), she made headlines again when she committed herself to a mental hospital to be with her female lover.

In 1985 Schneider did talk again about her experience on *Last Tango* to the press. To the *Daily Mail* (22 May), she said, 'I was exploited in every possible way. … I said things in the certainty that people wouldn't believe and, naturally, they did. … If I had known what [the film] would bring down on my head, I wouldn't have done it.' Schneider has continued to take small roles in European films, but few have been exhibited outside their countries of origin. She appeared briefly in the shadows in the Moroccan sequence of Cyril Collard's *Les Nuits fauves*

(*Wild Nights*, 1992), and was Rochester's terrible secret in the attic in
Franco Zefferelli's film of *Jane Eyre* (1996). While she has physically
survived hard times, her career has steadily continued in low gear, and
perhaps, after all, she no longer cares so much. She remains proud of her
work in *The Passenger*, but refuses to see much merit in *Last Tango*. To
have survived that period in her life may be enough. After all, she told
The New York Times back in 1973 that, 'I have a feeling that, like James
Dean, my destiny could be death. I keep thinking that I am going to die
young, in a car accident, like he did. … It's just a feeling that I've got
because I've done so much in such a short, short time.'[30]

The Passenger

8 Jean-Pierre/Tom

Just as the division between the movie actor Brando and the fictional character Paul is a blurred line, so the wannabe film director Tom is inextricably tied to the actor who incarnates him, Jean-Pierre Léaud. But while Brando is a universal icon, a star who shook up Hollywood and then was consumed by it, Léaud inhabits a more select, private corner of the collective memory of cinema, that of the French *nouvelle vague* and its ardent disciple, the cinephile.

The *nouvelle vague* – whose élite comprised Jean-Luc Godard, François Truffaut, Claude Chabrol, Jacques Rivette and Eric Rohmer – were all united in their cinephilia. Their background was as critics on *Cahiers du cinéma*, and their love of cinema was nurtured by visits to that esteemed temple of the seventh art, the Cinémathèque Française. Bertolucci felt a special kinship with this tendency, even at one stage in his career insisting on giving interviews in French as the true language of cinema.

In *Before the Revolution*, one of the hero Fabrizio's close friends is played by Bertolucci's one-time collaborator (and future director himself)

Tom as director

Gianni Amico as the semi-fictional embodiment of the director's own cinephilia. He claims to have seen *Vertigo* eight times, and *Voyage in Italy* fifteen. Against a backdrop of a poster of Jean-Luc Godard's *Une Femme est une femme*, he drops names of directors and intones sentences that echo Godard himself: 'Cinema is a matter of style, and style is a moral fact,' or 'Remember, Fabrizio! One cannot live without Rossellini!' Although Godard was only a decade older than Bertolucci, he had become a father figure who, in true Oedipal fashion, the younger man would have to discard. Godard's anarchic gestures – jump-cuts, heightened colour effects, disruptions of filmic conventions of time and space – would find their place in Bertolucci's stylistic formation. But they would be fused with the young Italian's extreme deployment of the camera as a manifestation of desire through movement and composition, harking back to earlier models such as Orson Welles and Max Ophuls.

By the time of *The Conformist*, Bertolucci was ready to leave Godard behind. While the French director was retreating more and more defensively into an analytical, semi-underground form of cinema in which pleasure in the spectacle would be replaced by ideological enquiry, the Italian director was discovering a way to reach a wider audience through greater sensuousness in his direction and more traditional forms of storytelling. Bertolucci would wickedly reveal that the address and telephone number given for Professor Quadri, the assassin's target in *The Conformist*, in reality belonged to Godard – a symbolic gesture as close to murder on a Greek highway as one can imagine.

So it was that many interpreted Tom in *Last Tango* to be a Godard surrogate. It would, however, take a very vague idea of Godard's methods to read Tom's clumsy efforts as related to any of the French director's work, accessible or otherwise. Tom is, after all, fulfilling a commission from television, and naïvely seeks to give Jeanne the aura of a Hollywood star. If there is a direct connection with Godard, it is in relation to his adoration of his first wife Anna Karina in his films of the early 60s, and especially of the scene in *Le Petit soldat* (1960) in which she becomes frozen in still frames as her lover celebrates her beauty. As David Thomson has reflected in his *Biographical Dictionary of Film*, 'It was the discovery that [Godard] loved Karina more in moving images than in life that may have broken their marriage.'

On the evidence of what we see of the shoot, however, Tom and his crew are far from competent in their craft. When they are in the house interviewing Jeanne about her childhood, her nurse interjects sour asides from time to time, but the camera always swings round too late to capture her on film. Bertolucci adds a sly joke at the crew's expense on the soundtrack when, in the first encounter at the railway station, Jeanne puts her hand down on their microphone, and the film sound is briefly lost. It was reported that at one stage of the editing Bertolucci considered incorporating the 16mm footage shot by Tom's crew within the film, but he abandoned this idea, and the dip in the sound is all that remains of such an intervention (now, of course, the use of video footage shot by a character within a film has become a cliché; Bertolucci used the device himself at the beginning of *Stealing Beauty*).

If Tom is almost certainly an incompetent technician, he is nevertheless consumed by the process of film-making as a way of seeing the world. When Jeanne appears at her family home, Tom's first concern is that she has changed her hairstyle – what about the continuity? (Whether this was also of concern to Bertolucci, the director cannot recall.) His passion is for the extravagant shot. He imagines a sweeping crane shot (which his crew are patently ill-equipped to perform) to discover her at the entrance to the courtyard, set to the elegiac accompaniment of Mozart on his portable tape machine (a camera movement that could be straight out of Bertolucci's own repertory). He opens one set of doors after another (remember the dream sequence in Hitchcock's *Spellbound*?) in adjoining rooms in Jeanne's childhood home. And when he finds Jeanne in the Metro, he frames her with his fingers even in the heat of an argument. He is directing life before he has learned how to live it.

It was a kind of making fun, a teasing of all the cinephiles of the world. It was an attempt to take a step out of cinephilia, so it was especially making fun of myself. But at the same time as being detached from this cinephilia, there was a lot of love for it. Since there had already been some ten or fifteen years of it, we could allow ourselves that. The Léaud character was really not seeing the reality of things, but seeing everything like a movie. He behaves a bit like a fool in some ways. It was also a kind of homage to Antoine Doinel and the Truffaut–Godard characters he played.

Born in 1944 to parents with a theatrical background, the teenage Jean-Pierre Léaud's future was sealed when he answered an ad in *France-Soir* for a teenage boy to act the semi-autobiographical role of Antoine Doinel in François Truffaut's first feature, *Les Quatre cents coups* (1958). At the age of fourteen, the film and Léaud became the toast of the 1959 Cannes Film Festival, and Truffaut of course became one of the foremost directors of the *nouvelle vague*. With Truffaut returning to the impish Doinel character at different stages of his life, Léaud would find his maturation from adolescent to adulthood mapped out on screen; as a clumsy teenage lover in *Antoine et Collette* (1961), as a young man struggling with employment in *Baisers volés* (1968), marriage and parenthood in *Domicile conjugal* (1970), and finally, in a slighter film

Les Quatre cents coups

which summed up all that had gone before in his life, *L'Amour en fuite* (1978). By its very nature, the role brought its own difficulties as the cycle progressed, for Léaud's Peter Pan quality – the troubled, often frantic adolescent who fails to grow up – began to lose its charm. But Léaud's close association with Truffaut also extended to other, ultimately more challenging roles, especially in *Les Deux Anglaises et le continent* (1971) and – most troublingly – as the petulant, emotionally insecure actor in the film-within-a-film in *La Nuit Américaine* (*Day for Night*, 1973).

In its early stages the relationship between Léaud and Truffaut involved the director taking on a parental responsibility, keeping the juvenile actor on a retainer so that he would always be available to him, and tending to his domestic needs. Such early dependency took its toll when Truffaut died in 1984 and Léaud suffered a breakdown. He was sighted wandering the streets talking to himself, sitting alone in cafés, and he appeared never to have any money. In 1986 he was even arrested for attacking an eighty-year-old woman neighbour with a pot of geraniums because he thought she was spying on him. Subsequently

Masculin-Féminin

Léaud has found his niche again in French cinema playing middle-aged roles, facing up to his true age with his now sullen features and portly figure. But if he was indelibly associated with Truffaut's first creation, he would take on very different parts for many of the major European directors of the 60s and 70s such as Pasolini or Rivette, and most memorably as the self-obsessed bohemian greedy for female companionship in Jean Eustache's masterpiece *La Maman et la putain* (1973).

Curiously, in an otherwise rather abortive interview with Andrew Sarris in *The Village Voice* in 1985, Léaud confessed that the best director he had worked with was Jean-Luc Godard. For Godard, the paranoid, manic Léaud was the perfect embodiment of that 'generation of Marx and Coca-Cola' portrayed in *Masculin-Féminin* (1965) and *La Chinoise* (1967). And time has shown that while Truffaut remained stylistically fixed in his neo Renoirian literary tales of tortured romance, it was Godard who broke through the forms and allowed his actors greater liberty. With Godard, Léaud was free to be himself, a true Parisian sprite whose manic energy and lack of worldliness would be affectionately mocked by Bertolucci, as he puckishly zips up his jacket and waves his hands in the air. And because of the way the shoot of *Last Tango* was scheduled, he was destined to remain in his own story, and would never observe any of the scenes involving Brando.

Jean-Pierre never met Marlon. He would say, 'Je suis l'acteur de Samedi,' because he was always shooting on Saturday when Marlon wasn't available. Actually he was glad, because he was terrified at the idea of meeting Brando.

9 The Aftermath

I attempted in *Last Tango* to marry Hollywood cinema to European cinema …
Brando with Schneider, lighting and precise camera movement with cinéma
vérité, script with improvisation, elaborate decor with a wild way of shooting, a
Hitchcock-type soundtrack with Gato Barbieri's tango. Like most Communist
intellectuals in Europe, I am condemned to be divided. I have a split personality
and the real contradiction within me is that I cannot quite synchronise my heart
and my brain. One of the two is always ahead of the other one.[31]

Thus spoke Bernardo Bertolucci in 1973, rationalising just what *Last
Tango* had meant to him artistically. If he had been a darling of the art
film circuit prior to this moment, now he had become virtually a
household name. *Last Tango* was really as far as he could take the
repeated pattern of his early films, with their protagonists torn between
dangerous, impulsive affairs and the safety of a bourgeois marriage.
Bertolucci's own long-term relationship did come to an end, though he
was to embark on a new one with one of his collaborators on *Novecento*,
Clare Peploe, who he married in 1980.

The commercial success of *Last Tango* enabled his producer Alberto
Grimaldi to bring together two American studios – Paramount and Fox –
to finance the epic *Novecento*, which covered the peasant revolution in
Parma in the first half of this century. Again he combined American and
European actors – Robert De Niro and Burt Lancaster, Dominique
Sanda and Gérard Depardieu. Bertolucci said of the young Depardieu,
'He fills the space like a young Marlon'.[32] As Gilbert Adair has observed
in *Flickers*, today a part like Paul in *Last Tango* 'would be given,
automatically, to Gérard Depardieu'. However, in *Novecento* the
reintroduction of explicitly political content into the more naturalistic
style that he had achieved in *Last Tango* proved problematic on all sides.

In his next film, *La Luna* (1979), Bertolucci returned to a
psychoanalytical cinema, this time serving up the taboos of heroin
addiction and incest between an opera diva and her teenage son. An
early sequence in the film picked up where *Last Tango* had left off, with

stepfather Douglas (Fred Gwynne) standing on his apartment balcony removing the chewing gum left behind by the dying Paul. There was also an echo of Jeanne in the appearance of the boy's Italian girlfriend Arianna, who sports a generous head of curls. But for all its pleasures, the film was less successful than *Last Tango* in its integration of an American star (Jill Clayburgh) into a largely European context, and failed to entice the audience into cinemas the way the earlier film had.

After the failure of *Tragedy of a Ridiculous Man* (1981), Bertolucci retreated from Italy, but in finding a sympathetic producer in Jeremy Thomas, he then embarked on what has become known as his 'exotic trilogy': the Oscar-garlanded *The Last Emperor* (1987), the Paul Bowles adaptation, *The Sheltering Sky* (1990), and *Little Buddha* (1993). *The Sheltering Sky* was something of a reverse mirror of *Last Tango*, with its central couple finding their relationship disintegrating in the vast open space of the Sahara. In 1995, Bertolucci finally returned to Italy to make *Stealing Beauty* (1996), about a young American girl in Tuscany discovering the identity of her real father as well as losing her virginity – a far sunnier portrait of young womanhood than *Last Tango*.

The production team of *Last Tango* were soon picked up by Hollywood. Vittorio Storaro won Oscars for his cinematography on Francis Ford Coppola's *Apocalypse Now!* (1976) and on Warren Beatty's *Reds* (1981), and continued his assocation with these directors on *One From the Heart* (1982) and *Dick Tracy* (1990). He has now begun collaborating with Carlos Saura, including a film project on the tango. Ferdinando Scarfiotti was specially chosen by Paul Schrader to design the highly sophisticated environments for *American Gigolo* (1980) and *Cat People* (1982), and just before his death was responsible for the fantasy world of Barry Levinson's *Toys* (1992). Another fatality should be recorded; Franco 'Kim' Arcalli died after working with Bertolucci on the screenplay and editing of *Novecento*.

The subsequent careers of Maria Schneider and Jean-Pierre Léaud have already been mentioned in the previous chapters. Marlon Brando went into retreat after *Last Tango*, seemingly bruised by the experience. According to Bertolucci, 'At the end of the movie he told me, "I will never make a film like this one again. I don't like being an actor at the best of times but it's never been this bad. I felt violated from the beginning to the end, every day and at every moment. I felt that my whole life, my most intimate feelings and even my children had been torn from within me".'[33] Brando elaborated on this himself in his autobiography: '*Last Tango* left me depleted and exhausted, perhaps in part because I'd done what Bernardo asked and some of the pain I was experiencing was my very own. Thereafter I decided to make my living in a way that was less devastating emotionally. In subsequent pictures I stopped trying to experience the emotions of my characters as I had always done before, and simply to act the part in a technical way.' True to his word, Brando has now fallen back on playing occasional character parts. Family tragedy has also taken its toll, with the imprisonment of his son Christian for manslaughter, and the suicide of his daughter Cheyenne.

In the 1990s Bertolucci was gradually to make contact with Brando again by telephone, and eventually visited him in at his Beverly Hills home. They talked just as they had in 1972 about personal matters, and then the conversation turned to *Last Tango*.

I told him I thought in *Last Tango* he had taken off his mask. His reply was, 'You really think that was me?' It was like when Jeanne tells Paul she has trapped him into talking about his past, and he replies,'Think I was telling you the truth? Maybe, maybe … '

And what is the legacy of *Last Tango* in the cinema? Obviously it set new levels of permissiveness on the screen, although more by reputation than anything else. But while even mainstream films may now boast greater sexual explicitness, few directors have entered this arena and captured anything like the Bataillesque intensity and fetid atmosphere of *Last Tango*.

The most obvious 'son of' *Last Tango* was Liliana Cavani's *The Night Porter* (1973), which starred Dirk Bogarde and Charlotte Rampling re-enacting, in a Viennese hotel room, a sadomasochistic relationship

The Night Porter

Ai No Corrida

they had begun in a concentration camp. Like *Last Tango*, there was a considerable age difference between the couple, and the sex between them involved a degree of pain and aggression (Bogarde walking barefoot on broken glass, thrusting his fingers in Rampling's mouth). The film had its defenders (and interestingly it shared one credit with *Last Tango*, the editor Franco Arcalli), but the crudity of Cavani's direction and a lurid voyeurism in the flashbacks to the camp made the result artistically dubious, to say the least. A more significant heir to *Last Tango* was Nagisa Oshima's *Ai no Corrida* (*L'Empire des sens/In the Realm of the Senses*, 1976), which as Bertolucci has observed shares Bataille as a source of inspiration. Oshima's film is, however, based on a true story of two lovers who become so sexually obsessed that they shut themselves off from the world. Oshima also went further than Bertolucci by having his actors perform real sex in front of the camera. Consequently the film pushed the pornography debate to the limit, and for all the critical acclaim it received, it could never achieve the wide distribution or commercial success of *Last Tango*.

What had by now become a minor genre in itself – tales of erotic obsession taken to perverse extremes – reached its nadir with Adrian Lyne's *9½ Weeks* (1985), a glossy charade in which a lubricious Mickey Rourke played kinky games with a compliant Kim Basinger. Louis Malle attempted to join the club with *Damage* (1992), but he was clearly uncomfortable working in Britain, and his cast never achieved the on-screen chemistry that had made *Last Tango* so compelling.

Even if it is thematically very different, one film that has approached the impact of *Last Tango* is David Cronenberg's *Crash* (1996). An adaptation of J.G. Ballard's novel of the same title, it deals with a group of people whose jaded sexual appetites can only be satisfied by their involvement in road accidents. Judging by the reaction of the moral watchdogs, and the problems it has caused the BBFC (who finally passed it uncut), it is a film capable of upsetting repressed sensibilities in a way that is amazingly reminiscent of the reception accorded *Last Tango*. Bertolucci himself has praised the film in *Film Comment* magazine's 'Guilty Pleasures' column: 'It's the first one of a long series, I hope, of *contes morales pour nous.* It is a completely pornographic film because there's no story and the characters are defined not by their psychologies but by their sexualities. But it is done in a kind of really extraordinarily serious way – *grave, solennel.*'[34] That description sounds remarkably like the kind of relationship that Paul desired from Jeanne – sex without social compromise. But then it still takes two to tango.

Notes

The main interview with Bernardo Bertolucci was conducted by the author in London in January 1996.

1 Don Ranvand and Enzo Ungari, *Bertolucci on Bertolucci.*

2 Guy Flatley, 'Bertolucci is All Tangoed Out', *The New York Times*, 11 February 1973.

3 Molly Haskell, 'Redeeming the Sordid – Inevitably', *The Village Voice*, 26 October 1972.

4 Charles Michener, 'Tango: The Hottest Movie', *Newseek*, 12 February 1973.

5 Pauline Kael, 'Tango', *The New Yorker*, 28 October 1972.

6 'Self-portrait of an Angel and Monster', *Time*, 22 January 1973.

7 Peter Manso, *Brando.*

8 Dennis Schaefer & Larry Salvato, 'Writing With Light', *Post Script* vol. 14 no. 1, Autumn 1984.

9 Marina Warner, 'Bertolucci the Non-Conformist', *Vogue* (U.K.), June 1972.

10 *Bertolucci on Bertolucci.*

11 Ibid.

12 'Bertolucci is All Tangoed Out'.

13 Ibid.

14 *Bertolucci on Bertolucci*.

15 Chris Hodenfield, 'Mondo Brando', *Rolling Stone*, 20 May 1976.

16 Joseph Gelmis, *The Film Director as Superstar.*

17 Mel Gussow, 'Bertolucci Indicts *Last Tango* Indictment as Obscene', *The New York Times*, 2 February 1973.

18 'Bertolucci is All Tangoed Out'.

19 Judy Klemesrud, 'Maria Says Her Tango is Not Blue', *The New York Times,* 4 February 1973.

20 Ibid.

21 'Tango', *The New Yorker*.

22 *Bertolucci on Bertolucci*.

23 'Maria Says Her Tango is Not Blue'.

24 Ibid.

25 Ibid.

26 Frank Segers, 'Make it a Boy, Film Makes Sense', *Variety*, 6 February 1974.

27 'Maria Says Her Tango is Not Blue'.

28 Ibid.

29 James Fox, 'The Next Tango', *The Sunday Times Magazine*, 9 February 1973.

30 'Maria Says Her Tango is Not Blue'.

31 'Bertolucci is All Tangoed Out'.

32 'The Next Tango'.

33 *Bertolucci on Bertolucci*.

34 Bernardo Bertolucci, 'Guilty Pleasures', *Film Comment*, July/August 1996.

Credits

LAST TANGO IN PARIS
(L'Ultimo Tango A Parigi)
Italy/France 1972

Director
Bernardo Bertolucci
Production companies
PEA
Produzioni Europée
Associates s.a.s – Rome
Les Productions Artistes
Associés s.a. – Paris
Producer
Alberto Grimaldi
Story
Bernardo Bertolucci
Screenplay
Bernardo Bertolucci
Franco Arcalli
Adaptation, French
dialogue
Agnès Varda
Director of photography
Vittorio Storaro
Editor
Franco Arcalli
in collaboration with
Roberto Perpignani
Supervision of set
design
Ferdinando Scarfiotti
Set designer and Set
dresser
Maria Paola Maino
Costumes
Gitt Magrini
Music composed by
Gato Barbieri
Music arranged and
conducted by
Oliver Nelson

Production manager
Mario Di Biase
Production manager for
France
Gérard Crosnier
Assistant production
manager
Francis Peltier
Production supervisor
Enzo Provenzale
Sound engineer
Antoine Bonfanti
Cameraman
Enrico Umetelli
Assistant cameramen
Luigi Bernardini
Mauro Marchetti
Gaffer
Luciano Galli
Key grip
Alfredo Marchetti
Script supervisor
Suzanne Durremberger
Assistant director
Fernand Moszkowicz
Second assistant
director
Jean-David Lefebvre
Still photographer
Angelo Novi
Assistant editor
Gabriela Cristiani
Production secretary
Ginette Mejinsky
Assistant set designer
Albert Rajau
Make-up
Maud Regon
Hair dressing
José Cecchini

Production accountants
José Lichtig
Maurizio Forti
Post-production
supervision
Enzo Ocone
Sound editor
Michael Billingsley
English version mixing
by
Fausto Ancillai
Printing supervised by
Ernesto Novelli

129 minutes
11,607 feet

Marlon Brando
Paul
Maria Schneider
Jeanne
Jean-Pierre Léaud
Tom
Darling Legitimus
Concierge
Catherine Sola
TV Script-girl
Mauro Marchetti
TV Cameraman
Dan Diament
TV Sound Engineer
Peter Schommer
TV Assistant Cameraman
Catherine Allégret
Catherine
Marie-Hélène Breillat
Monique
Catherine Breillat
Mouchette
Stéphane Kosiak
Small Removal Man

Gérard Lepennec
Tall Removal Man
Maria Michi
Rosa's Mother
Rosa
Veronica Lazare
Luce Marquand
Olympia
Massimo Girotti
Marcel
Giovanna Galetti
Prostitute
Arman Ablanalp
Prostitute's Customer
Gitt Magrini
Jeanne's Mother
Mimi Pinson
President of Tango Jury
Ramon Mendizabal
Tango Orchestra Leader

Cut from final version:
Michel Delahaye
Bible Salesman
Laura Betti
Miss Blandish
Jean-Luc Bideau
Barge Captain

Music note: the soundtrack was recorded in the summer of 1972 in New York, with a jazz ensemble featuring Barbieri on tenor sax, Joachim Kuhn on piano, Charlie Hayden on bass and Daniel Humair on drums, as well as a full string orchestra, Brazilian congo players, and specialist bandoneon players for the tango numbers. However, the tracks heard on the Grammy Award-winning, best-selling 'original motion picture score' album were from separate sessions held in Rome in November featuring mainly Italian musicians.

Credits checked by Markku Salmi, BFI Filmographic Unit.

Bibliography

Adair, Gilbert, *Flickers* (London: Faber and Faber, 1995).

Alley, Robert, *Last Tango in Paris* (novelisation) (New York: Dell Books, 1973).

Bataille, Georges, *Blue of Noon* (translated by Harry Mathews) (London: Marion Boyars, 1979).

Bertolucci, Bernardo, *Last Tango in Paris* (screenplay plus essays by Pauline Kael and Norman Mailer) (London: Plexus, 1976).

Brando, Marlon with Lindsey, Robert, *Brando: Songs My Mother Taught Me* (London: Century Press, 1994).

Carroll, Kent E. (ed), *Close Up: Last Tango in Paris* (New York: Grove Press, 1973).

Dewe Matthews, Tom, *Censored* (London: Chatto & Windus, 1994).

Gelmis, Joseph, *The Film Director as Superstar* (London: Secker & Warburg, 1970).

Grobel, Lawrence, *Conversations With Marlon Brando* (London: Bloomsbury, 1978).

Haskell, Molly, *From Reverence to Rape: The Treatment of Women in the Movies* (Chicago: University of Chicago Press, 1987).

Kline, T. Jefferson, *Bertolucci's Dream Loom: A Psychoanalytic Study of Cinema* (Amherst: University of Massachusetts Press, 1987).

Kolker, Robert Phillip, *Bernardo Bertolucci* (London: British Film Institute, 1985).

Manso, Peter, *Brando* (London: Weidenfeld & Nicolson, 1994).

Peary, Danny (ed) *Cult Movies 2* (New York: Dell Publishing, 1983).

Ranvaud, Don and Ungari, Enzo, *Bertolucci on Bertolucci* (London: Plexus, 1982).

Roud, Richard (ed), *A Critical Dictionary of the Cinema* (London: Secker & Warburg, 1982).

Russell, John, *Francis Bacon* (London: Thames and Hudson, 1993).

Ryan, Paul, *Marlon Brando: A Portrait* (London: Plexus, 1992).

Thomson, David, *A Biographical Dictionary of Film* (London: Secker & Warburg, 1994).

Tonetti, Claretta Micheletti, *Bernardo Bertolucci* (New York: Twayne Publishers, 1995).

Key Articles and Interviews

Bachman, Gideon, 'Every Sexual Relationship is Condemned', *Film Quarterly* vol. 26 no. 3, Spring 1973.

Barr, Alan, 'The Better to See … Improbable Vision in *Last Tango in Paris'*, *Film Criticism* vol. 7 no. 2, Winter 1983.

Cott, Jonathan, 'A Conversation with Bernardo Bertolucci', *Rolling Stone*, 21 June 1973.

Dawson, Jan, '*Last Tango in Paris'*, *Monthly Film Bulletin*, May 1973.

Kinder, Marshe and Houston, Beverle, 'Bertolucci and the Dance of Danger', *Sight and Sound*, Autumn 1973.

Mellen, Joan, 'Sexual Politics and *Last Tango in Paris'*, *Film Quarterly* vol. 26 no. 3, Spring 1973.

Phelps, Guy, 'Censorship and the Press', *Sight and Sound*, Summer 1973.

Rice, Julian C., 'Bertolucci's *Last Tango in Paris'*, *Journal of Popular Film* vol. 3 no. 2, Spring 1974.

BFI Film Classics '... could scarcely be improved upon ... informative, intelligent, jargon-free companions.'
The Observer

Each book in the BFI Publishing Film Classics series honours a great film from the history of world cinema. With new titles published each year, the series is rapidly building into a collection representing some of the best writing on film. If you would like to receive further information about future Film Classics or about other books on film, media and popular culture from BFI Publishing, please fill in your name and address and return this card to the BFI*.

No stamp is needed if posted in the UK, Channel Islands, or Isle of Man.

_____

NAME

_____

ADDRESS

_____

_____

POSTCODE

_____

*North America: Please return your card to:
Indiana University Press, Attn: LPB, 601 N Morton Street,
Bloomington, IN 47401-3797

BFI Publishing
21 Stephen Street
FREEPOST 7
LONDON
W1E 4AN